The credit con desktop guide

second edition

Roger Mason

THOROGOOD

First published by Hawksmere plc in 1999.
Updated and reprinted in 2004 by
Thorogood Publishing Ltd
10-12 Rivington Street
London EC2A 3DU
Telephone: 020 7749 4748
Fax: 020 7729 6110
Email: info@thorogood.ws
Web: www.thorogood.ws

Crown copyright is reproduced with the permission
of the Controller of Her Majesty's Stationery Office.

A CIP catalogue record for this book is
available from the British Library.

ISBN 1 85418 299 4
Printed by Replika Press.

Designed and typeset by Driftdesign.

CONTENTS

Icons

Throughout the Desktop Guide series of books you will see references and symbols in the margins. These are designed for ease of use and quick reference directing you to key features of the text. The symbols used are:

 definition

 question and answer

 for example

 checklist

Introduction

It is universally recognised that the payment culture in Britain is bad. Other countries have problems too, but foreign managers coming here sometimes find that a cultural adjustment has to be made. Slow payment is unfair, immoral, bad for small businesses and bad for the national economy. Everyone agrees that something should be done.

Government has taken two significant steps to try and secure a big improvement. The first is the Late Payment of Commercial Debts (Interest) Act 1998. This provides for statutory interest and is introduced in stages up to 1st November 2002. This is controversial and just might make things worse. But we wish the measure well and will watch the results very closely.

The second step is fundamental changes to the way that the courts operate and these changes took effect from 26th April 1999. The aim is to make justice more speedy and more certain. It is too soon to see the results, but the changes should help and are most welcome. Again, we will watch the results closely.

The main contribution has to come from effective management, and the role of credit controllers is vital. The status of credit managers has increased in recent years and there is greater recognition of the importance of the work that they do. Both improvements are justified. This Guide is designed to help them and everyone involved in this demanding task.

There is a lot of advice in this book. I hope that you will find it all interesting and will follow quite a bit of it. Do not on any account follow all of it. If you do, you will finish up with superb credit control and perhaps not too much business. Credit control is a very practical matter and the commercial realities must always be remembered.

You should treat this book as a menu and select the parts that are most relevant to you. In anticipation that many readers will do this I have covered some topics in more than one chapter. This is not in order to pad the book, but because they affect more than one subject.

The book deals with the legal system in England and Wales. Scottish law has many similarities, but there are differences. Please keep this in mind if your problem is a legal one.

The legal chapters go beyond a basic introduction, but space limitations prevent them being a comprehensive Do-It-Yourself guide. They do completely cover some but cannot cover all aspects.

I have practised credit control for many years and this book draws on some of my experiences. Sometimes I write in the first person and the book is less impersonal than many that are available. I trust that this is understood and adds to the practical usefulness.

I have generally followed the fast-disappearing practice of using the word 'he' rather then 'he or she', or some gender-neutral word. This is because to use 'he or she' hundreds of times seems contrived. Women readers should please know that my words are intended to encompass them equally. In some places I have assumed an organisation or a major company. Many readers will work for such an employer, but it is the ideas that are important. They can just as well be used by a one-man (or one-woman) business.

Finally, a message to nearly everyone who reads these words. You are on the side of the angels and deserve every success. My best wishes to you.

Roger Mason

1

chapter one

The cost of credit

Introduction

There is no law, legal or moral, that states that credit must be granted. Credit only applies if the seller accepts it or fails to stop the purchaser taking it anyway. It is worth asking yourself whether or not credit should be granted at all. In most cases the answer is a self evident 'yes', because sales would be difficult or impossible without it. Nevertheless, do ask the question. Just possibly, you should not be giving credit at all.

It is interesting to work out the true cost of credit but there are very practical reasons why you should have the information at your fingertips. The knowledge will concentrate your mind and it will help you decide whether alternative courses of action are worth pursuing.

Vigorous collection policies may cost sales (or so you may be told). How many sales and is the profit on these sales more or less than the cost of the credit? Are some of these sales ones that you would be better off not having?

Let us say that it is 2 pm on a Friday. The use of a motorbike despatch rider would mean that you could collect a cheque and get it into your bank that day. Would the cost of doing it be more or less than the money saved?

There are three elements of cost that can be precisely calculated, and others that although real are more difficult to quantify.

Cost

The three measurable elements of the cost

1   Interest paid or not received

Most businesses operate with an overdraft and the rate of interest paid to the bank is a key element of the cost of the credit. There is still a cost if the business does not have an overdraft. This is because it will be losing the interest it would have received through having the money in a deposit account or otherwise invested.

Let us consider a business paying 10% on money borrowed. Every £100,000 borrowed will cost £833.33 per month, £192.31 per week and £27.40 per day in bank interest.

The calculation for a day is $\dfrac{£100,000 \times 10\%}{365} = £27.40$

If the bank debits interest more frequently than once a year the rate over a period is rather more than 10%. If interest is debited quarterly the interest over a year adds to £10,381 rather than £10,000.

2   Depreciating currency

Due to inflation money banked after a period of credit does not have the same purchasing power as money banked at the time of delivery of the goods or services.

Let us return to the same £100,000 invoice and assume that inflation is 3% p.a. Depreciating currency will cost £250.00 per month, £57.69 per week and £8.22 per day.

The calculation for a day is $\dfrac{£100,000 \times 3\%}{365} = £8.22$

It has not been seen in Britain since the 1930s but appreciating currency (deflation) is possible and some commentators think it could recur. Were it to do so there would be a benefit in being owed money, so long of course as payment was ultimately received.

3   Financing VAT

Some businesses do not pay VAT and for them financing it does not apply. However, it is a factor for all businesses that do pay. The VAT part of an invoice must be financed in exactly the same way as the rest of the invoice. This is so whether the business is registered under one of the cash schemes or whether it pays based on invoice dates.

If a cash scheme does not apply, the VAT is normally payable on average 75 days after raising the invoice. For example, all invoices dated between January 1st and March 31st contribute to a VAT payment which must reach Customs and Excise by April 30th. This is 75 days after the midpoint of the quarter. It is tempting, but of course wrong, to say that nothing is lost provided that the money is received before the VAT payment is due. A day's interest saved is always a day's interest saved. If you can get paid in three days instead of four, the one day saved is worth exactly the same as the one day saved from 76 to 75.

Let us return to the same £100,000 invoice. It will probably carry VAT of 17.5% and be for a total of £117,500. Assuming a 10% borrowing rate, each day's improvement will save £4.79 on the VAT part.

The calculation is $\dfrac{\text{£17,500 x 10\%}}{365} = \text{£4.79}$

A practical example

The above is straightforward and should be readily understood. You might like to check your understanding by working out the cost of a day's credit in the following example. The calculation is given at the end of this chapter, immediately before 'Checklist'.

Your business is owed £1,000,000 plus 17.5% VAT (£1,175,000 in total). You pay 12% interest on your bank overdraft and the inflation rate is 6% p.a.

The other elements of the cost

The following are difficult or impossible to measure, but they are very real and should not be overlooked.

1 The cost of administration

You will have to send out statements, make telephone calls and write letters, administer a sales ledger, answer questions from auditors and so on. In addition there is the cost of management time which can be very high. Many people underestimate the true cost of administration.

2 Increased risk of bad debts

There is often a close correlation between the age of a debt and the chances of it turning into a bad debt. The fact that a debt is overdue may indicate that a customer has a problem paying. It may of course also indicate that he does not want to pay, or that there is some administrative problem holding up payment. A customer may be sound at the time of delivery and sound at the limit of the agreed credit terms. But a change in fortunes may cause a problem after this period.

Remember also that if there is continuous trading the loss will be greater if a long period of credit is allowed and the customer then fails. If the trade is £1,000 a month, the loss cannot be more than £1,000 if 30 days credit is enforced. If six months credit is permitted the maximum loss is £6,000.

Accountants and auditors often recognise the relationship when drawing up a general reserve for bad debts. They typically use a formula such as the following:

0 – 30 days	NIL reserve
30 – 60 days	1% reserve
60 – 120 days	2% reserve
120 – 180 days	10% reserve
Over 180 days	50% reserve

3   Business failure

In extreme cases the very survival of the business can be at stake, and this can be the highest cost of all. A surprisingly high proportion of businesses that fold are making profits at the time of their failure. They are undercapitalised and failure can be caused by slow payment and liquidity problems.

You may well know at least one rather bitter person whose potentially successful business failed, either because of bad debts or because his customers took too long to pay. The business may well have been undercapitalised but nevertheless poor credit control probably contributed to the failure. If he had been able to solve the problem the business might have been saved. Such unfortunate people usually learn the lessons and get it right if they are able to start up again. How sad though that the cost of learning is so high.

4   Lost opportunity

In many businesses, funds are rationed. Even sound, profitable projects cannot be undertaken because the necessary finance just is not available. In these circumstances effective credit control can release funds to allow them to go ahead.

Possible savings related to profit

Quite startling results are often obtained when the cost of credit is compared with the net profit of a business. It is common for unauthorised credit to swallow up much of the net profit, and it can sometimes be the difference between a profit and a loss.

Suppose that unauthorised credit is taking 2% of turnover and suppose that net profit before tax is 2% of turnover. If the cost of unauthorised credit can be halved then there will be a 50% increase in net profit before tax. It may well require a very large increase in sales to achieve the same result.

Personal knowledge of the cost of credit

Before leaving this chapter you are strongly advised to work out the real cost of credit for your own business. It is best expressed as the saving that can be achieved in getting £1,000 in one day earlier. If you work for a large company perhaps you should make it £10,000 or even a larger figure. Please do the calculation for yourself, but you will probably find that the result is between 30 pence per thousand pounds per day and 45 pence per thousand pounds per day.

Having worked out the figure keep it in mind as you read this book and keep it in mind as you do your job. Tell your staff if you have any. Perhaps pin it up in the office. It will help you get your priorities right.

Answer to the practical example

This was given earlier in the chapter.

Cost of borrowing (£1,175,000 x 12% for 1 day)	£386.30
Cost of depreciating currency (£1,175,000 x 6% for 1 day)	£193.15
	£579.45

Checklist

✓ Do work out the real cost of credit for your own organisation. This is the most important piece of advice in Chapter 1.

✓ Do express it as the true daily cost of being owed £10,000 (or some such figure).

✓ Do memorise the result, tell other people, keep referring to it and use the information.

✓ Do remember that the risk of a bad debt, and the likely amount of a bad debt, both increase the longer that it is owing.

✓ Do work out the annual cost of giving credit in your organisation, and do compare it with the net profit of your organisation (if applicable). Do prepare to be surprised by the result.

✓ Do not underestimate the true cost of administration.

✓ Do remember that, for the purposes of the cost of credit, the date that you pay VAT to the government is irrelevant. A day's interest saved is always a day's interest saved.

chapter two

The right attitude
for credit control

Introduction

Generals throughout the ages have known that their troops will fight more effectively if they believe that God and the folks at home are on their side. This is another way of saying that soldiers fight best when they believe in the cause, and it is why an army of volunteers is usually better than an army of conscripts.

It is stretching the analogy a long way but it is true for business as well. No matter how well he is paid and trained, a salesman will do better if he believes that the product being sold really is excellent value for money. He tries harder and somehow the belief gets through to the customers. Similarly a person collecting debts will do best if he believes that he is a valuable member of the staff doing a vital job, and if he believes that the requests being made are entirely fair and reasonable. He should feel that his work is appreciated and that his bosses take an interest in it.

This seems blindingly obvious but it very often does not happen in practice. It is worth stating the points one by one:

- The collector is a valuable member of staff.

- The collector does a vital job.

- The requests being made are entirely fair and reasonable.

- The collector's work is appreciated.

- The collector's bosses take an interest in the work.

The first two points are always true. The third point should be true and usually is. The last two points should be true but may not be. It is up to management to see that they are.

Perhaps your staff need motivating and have difficulty getting into the right frame of mind. Perhaps this applies to you. The best results will be achieved when the collector is in a positive frame of mind and the first part of this chapter is devoted to helping you achieve this.

Some people find it helpful to have truisms pinned up in the office. Others keep certain phrases in mind and mutter them to themselves when the customers are being difficult. The following are all true and may be helpful:

- Credit is not a right – and even it if is, extra credit certainly is not a right.

- I am doing one of the most important jobs in the company.

- We are not a bank.

- We are not a registered charity.

- We are not a branch of the social services.

- We are not an agency of the Samaritans.

- There is no profit until the money is in the bank.

- The debtor does not belong to a protected species.

You have probably come across similar phrases that appeal to you. Mutter them under your breath when the going gets tough, particularly when you are subject to lies and abuse. In some circumstances it can be productive to say them to a customer, particularly if you can lighten the conversation in a jocular way. I have often told a customer that our banking licence has not yet come through, and gone on to offer an introduction to Barclays or National Westminster.

Often one of the phrases will be spontaneously adopted by almost the whole company. I know a company where this happened, '*There is no profit until the money is in the bank*'. Excited salesmen tell of a thrilling development but finish by saying with a smile 'but as we all know there is no profit until the money is in the bank'.

As in so many things, humour and a light touch are often the most effective approach. A sour-faced instruction from the Managing Director may well be resented. But a smiling request to write out a hundred lines '*There is no profit until the money is in the bank*' will probably be appreciated and make the same point.

If credit control is only part of your job there may be scope for doing it at a time when you feel at your best. If you always wake up feeling depressed and only get going after the sixth cup of black coffee, then perhaps you should be phoning customers from mid morning onwards. Full time credit specialists may not have this option but perhaps they could do the paperwork first thing. The way that a person is feeling really does communicate in subtle ways on the telephone, and this is discussed in more detail in Chapter 7 on the use of the telephone.

Of course you should on no account use this to put off what needs doing. Which brings us to one of the most important rules for effective credit control:

- **Ask early and ask often.**

If you have difficulty remembering this, think of the slogan that is said to circulate in Chicago on election days 'Vote early and vote often'. Remember, the earlier that you ask, the earlier that you are likely to be paid.

No effective collector gets very far without a sceptical attitude. However, you should not allow yourself to become too cynical, though it is true that much of your time will be devoted to people who give you problems. Some will behave in a very unfair way and a few may be downright dishonest.

Nevertheless, do not go sour on the human race and never forget the customers who do not give problems. As well as being spiritually uplifting this is sound practical advice. It normally pays to be friendly on the telephone, at least to start with. So remember that most of your customers are nice people, rather like you in fact. And like most nice people they resent being harassed in an unjustifiable way. You should give consideration to the good customers as well as chase the bad ones.

It may be difficult to believe but a few customers pay early and some will pay on time. A surprisingly high number of people settle their telephone account within 48 hours of receiving the invoice. Quite a lot of customers will pay shortly past the due date, even without being asked. Of the remainder, a few are probably rogues but some are probably just incompetent. Some may have very sad personal problems or difficulties with their businesses. They may be at risk of losing their businesses and perhaps even their houses and personal assets may be at stake.

The chapter, so far, covers attitudes and the correct approach for credit control and collecting. These are universal and useful for everyone involved. The concluding part is three matters that are mainly for management though they will be of interest to all.

Bonuses and commission for staff

In many companies credit staff do a job where results can be precisely measured and are closely linked to the efforts of identified individuals. This is particularly true if the credit staff are collecting a large spread of small debts. In these circumstances luck and special factors play less of a role and the efforts of the collectors will most likely correlate with the results achieved. These conditions may be suitable for the introduction of bonuses or commission for the collectors.

As with all bonus and commission schemes the best results will be obtained if management remembers three golden rules:

- Keep it fair.

- Keep it simple.

- Make the rewards big enough to motivate.

I formulate these rules based on much personal experience, but one situation in particular. As a young accountant I was once responsible for a wages department that paid out bonuses on a newly introduced incentive scheme. The bonuses were very small, unfair as between different recipients, difficult to calculate and almost impossible to check. They broke each of the three golden rules.

After two payments a trade union official visited me. With a broad smile he said that the people involved felt sorry for me. They had talked it over and wanted to save me a lot of unnecessary work. Accordingly they wanted the scheme stopped and a very small monthly donation made to a charity of the management's choosing. I had no part in devising the scheme but I have never forgotten the lessons.

Record the progress

A visual reminder of the target and daily progress helps wonderfully to concentrate minds, especially if bonuses are involved. There are many possibilities but the golden rule is **keep it simple**. The ideal is a chart that takes just a few seconds a day to update. The following is a good example of an effective chart and numerous offices benefit from something like it.

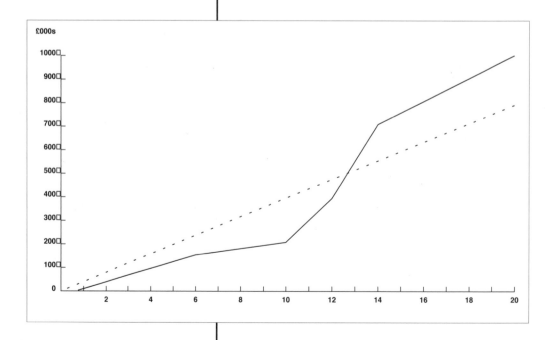

The target for the 20 day month has been set at £800,000 and the dotted line shows how the money should be coming in. This is drawn in at the beginning of the month whereas the solid line is updated daily to show the cumulative total actually received.

Staff motivation is likely to be best if the target is not easy but definitely achievable. Motivation also benefits if the target is set in consultation with staff and not just announced from on high.

Measure the results

It is highly desirable that you measure the results that you are achieving. If you do this you will be able to assess your performance and will be able to see if the position is improving or deteriorating. This is very important and a deteriorating position should be more worrying than an equally bad but static figure. The monthly sales ledger balance does not by itself give the complete information.

Many factors influence an assessment of the monthly sales ledger balance and especially relevant are the monthly invoicing figures. A company selling Christmas goods will probably have high sales ledger balances in October, November and December. This does not indicate poor credit control, just high invoicing in these three months. Quite probably a significant part of the overall balance is not yet even due for payment.

Numerous systems are used for measuring credit performance. Some are sophisticated and very complicated. They are designed for use in special situations but for most readers of this book they are unnecessary. It is better to adopt a simple system that can measure results in just a few minutes a month.

Whatever system you adopt it is important that you use the same one consistently. Only by comparing like with like will you be able to see if the position is improving or deteriorating. It is vital to spot developing trends.

The most commonly used system is one that measures the average number of days credit outstanding. I recommend it as a good compromise system for most businesses. It is best illustrated with an example:

	Net invoicing	Net cash receipts	Net sales ledger balance
Feb 28			£2,000,000
March	£950,000	£950,000	£2,000,000
April	£1,000,000	£800,000	£2,200,000
May	£1,200,000	£700,000	£2,700,000
June	£900,000	£1,300,000	£2,300,000

The average number of days credit at May 31 is calculated as follows:

Balance at May 31	£2,700,000	
Less May invoicing	£1,200,000	31 days
	£1,500,000	
Less April invoicing	£1,000,000	30 days
	£500,000	
Less March invoicing	£950,000	16 days
	NIL	77 days

The March calculation is $\dfrac{£500,000 \times 31}{£950,000} = 16$ days

The average number of days credit at June 30 is calculated as follows:

Balance at June 30	£2,300,000	
Less June invoicing	£900,000	30 days
	£1,400,000	
Less May invoicing	£1,200,000	31 days
	£200,000	
Less April invoicing	£1,000,000	16 days
	NIL	67 days

The April calculation is $\dfrac{£200,000 \times 30}{£1,000,000} = 6$ days

So in this example there has been a big improvement in the month of June.

Checklist

✓ Do remember that credit control and collection are vital jobs. Tell yourself, tell your staff and tell others. Nevertheless, remember that you cannot always have your own way. Other departments have needs as well.

✓ Do remember helpful truisms, especially witty ones. Perhaps pin them up.

✓ Do things that make you feel positive.

✓ Do not put off doing things. A good rule of thumb is *Ask Early, Ask Often*. The earlier you ask, the earlier you are likely to be paid.

✓ Do be sceptical, and perhaps very sceptical, but do not become totally cynical. Never forget the good customers and the good payers.

✓ Do record your progress. A simple system is usually the best.

✓ Do calculate the period of credit. A simple system is usually the best. Do calculate it regularly and do be consistent with the method.

✓ Do watch the trend in the period of credit. This is often more important then the raw figure.

chapter three

The right credit policies

Introduction

Does your company have credit policies? This may sound flippant but some do not, except of course a wish to be paid as quickly as possible and this to be achieved without asking the customer for payment. It is sometimes revealing to ask the question of both junior staff and senior staff in the same organisation. The junior staff are sometimes closer to the problems and may give a less flattering assessment. Junior staff sometimes ask questions beginning 'why don't they?'. Sadly, 'they' are often not the customers but the speaker's own managers and directors.

Credit policies should be well thought out, and very clear. It is helpful if they have general support throughout the organisation.

This does not mean that the credit controller should always get exactly what he wants. Some credit departments are much put upon, but occasionally they do overstate their case. Sales are very important too and other departments have legitimate concerns as well. It is vital that priorities are balanced. Writers and lecturers on credit control sometimes say that customers respect firm credit policies and that such policies do not result in lost sales. Sadly, the last point is not always true, though it is true that customers respect firm policies.

Credit policies should be widely discussed throughout the organisation. Everyone should be encouraged to put a constructive point of view. Decisions should then be made by senior management and should very clearly be made known. Finally, backing should be given to the people implementing the policies and not be withdrawn if problems follow. It is very unfair and demoralising if backing is not given.

Credit policies should be realistic. It is useless to have credit policies not based on reality and such policies have a demoralising effect on staff. Credit control is a demanding task and the people doing it need to feel that they have clear guidelines and the support of their bosses. This does not of course mean that policies cannot aspire to excellent results. For example the following meets the above criteria:

- Normal period of credit   30 days

- Internally accepted   40 days

- Serious concern   50 days

This means that the customer is told to pay within 30 days and that the credit controller has agreed leeway beyond this point, but not very much leeway.

There are no credit policies that are right for everyone all the time. Credit policies should be reviewed from time to time and changes made if necessary or desirable. It is a common mistake not to do this and to keep once excellent policies in place after conditions have changed. If your biggest competitor is giving six months interest-free credit the fact should not be ignored. Perhaps it is right to continue existing policies, but the point should be considered and a conscious decision made. All credit policies should be the result of conscious decisions that are reviewed from time to time.

The remainder of this chapter is devoted to an outline consideration of some of the main credit control policies that you should consider. Obviously, not everyone will be relevant to individual businesses and you should treat it like a menu – briefly look at them all, then concentrate on the ones that are relevant.

Credit

Should you give credit?

This may seem a silly question but do consider the point. If the answer is 'no' then this Guide may be one of the best investments that you have ever made.

Some businesses give credit because it is expected, or because they always have, or because competitors do, or because customers ask for it. These are all strong reasons but they are not necessarily conclusive. Do not think only about sales, think about what would happen to profits if credit was not given.

If credit was not given at all there would be no costs for preparing and posting statements, no costs for running a sales ledger and having it audited, no salaries for credit control staff, no costs of a credit control department and no credit control telephone costs. There would be no bad debts and no interest costs for the financing of debtors.

For the overwhelming majority of readers it is obvious that credit should be given, but not for all readers. Do not move on without considering the point.

What nominal period of credit is allowed?

This is a key question and it is very important that you do have a policy and communicate it to your customers. If you do not, then you have a policy by default. This is to accept whatever is the buyer's policy. You may be lucky but you very probably will not be.

Your policy will be influenced by the relative strength of your position, the attitude of competitors, the traditions and accepted practice in your industry, your need for extra sales, and so on. There are three cynical but practical reasons for making the nominal period of credit as short as possible:

- A very few customers will pay to terms, whatever they are. Believe it or not there are still one or two who will, unprompted, respond to seven day terms by posting a cheque on the sixth day. Admittedly, they may not operate in your sector. A slightly larger group will, unprompted, pay just after the nominally due date.

- Quite a large group of customers will take a fixed time beyond the nominal date, whatever it is. They have, for example, a cynical policy of taking an extra 30 days. If you specify seven days you will be paid after 37 days.

If you say 30 days, you will be paid after 60 days. If you say six months then seven months will be taken.

- Your collection procedures will be geared to the nominal due date and normally only start at this point. If you have an extended nominal period of credit then you are starting collecting late.

You should carefully consider the difference between a fixed number of days after invoice date and terms such as 'net monthly account'. They are sometimes wrongly taken to mean much the same thing. An invoice issued on April 8th, with 30 days terms, is due for payment on May 8th. The same invoice with 'net monthly account' is due at the end of the following month, namely May 30th. Monthly account gives an average of 15 days more than 30 day terms.

What actual period of credit is allowed?

Whatever collection methods are chosen, increasing pressure will be asserted. This will culminate in a refusal to make further supplies and normally it will eventually result in legal action to recover the debt. Exceptional circumstances may warrant exceptional actions, but you will usually have a policy for the broad mass of the unexceptional debts. Typically, this could be expressed as follows:

- Nominal term   30 days

- First letter   35 days

- Second letter   45 days

- Seven day warning letter
  and stop supplies   55 days

- Commence legal action   62 days

This is not a recommendation of this programme. Circumstances vary and you must design a plan to suit your business. It may be too tough or it may be too generous. In particular, you should consider whether two standard letters are desirable rather than just the one. If you are in a very strong position you will probably want to exploit it. For example, most oil companies insist that most garages pay for petrol by direct debit on seven day terms. Supplies are immediately cut off if payment is not made.

What sanctions will you use?

You will almost certainly face the problem of some customers being unable or unwilling to make payments in a time acceptable to you. Normal collection procedures will fail and very firm action will have to be taken. Some of the possibilities are one or more of the following:

- Cut off further supplies until payment has been made.

- Use a collection agency.

- Threaten legal action and then take it.

- Close the account and refuse further business.

- Write off the debt.

You will need to have a policy on who will decide and at what stage. Is the credit controller authorised to make the decisions alone or should others be involved?

Cutting off supplies may be devastating or it may not concern the buyer at all. In the last section it was mentioned that most garages have to pay for petrol by means of a seven day direct debit. Withdrawal of supplies (which is usually enforced) is crippling to the customer, especially as they are also placed on an industry blacklist. Garages only have storage capacity for a few days supply of petrol and are soon out of business.

Legal action and the cutting off of supplies are the most common sanctions and they usually work. But there are others, such as publicity or reporting a late payer to their trade association or professional body. Very often the threat is all that is needed. Most solicitors, for example, would take steps to avoid a complaint to the Law Society. This is so even though the Law Society would probably decline to get involved.

What collection methods do you use?

In most cases the methods will be a judicious mixture of letters and telephone calls. Each of these methods has a chapter devoted exclusively to them. Telephone calls are usually the most effective and much more effective than standard letters. However, cost and especially time limitations may make their use impractical. Telephone calls are most suitable for large and problem debts.

It may be wise to consider third-party collections, including credit agencies and factoring. There are separate chapters on each of these too. If you have high value invoices and large balances with a customer it becomes more economic to have personal visits, messenger collection and so on.

Do you use credit insurance?

Chapter 12 is devoted exclusively to this. If you do use credit insurance you will need a policy on whether to insure all debts or only some, perhaps the bigger ones.

Do you run status checks?

This is covered in Chapter 10 on credit agencies. It is also mentioned in Chapter 4 on opening a new account.

Do you operate credit limits?

This is covered in Chapter 4 on opening a new account.

What are your conditions of sale?

This is a big and important subject and Chapter 15 is devoted exclusively to it. Amongst the conditions to be considered are:

- Retention of title.

- Interest on overdue payments.

- Method of payment.

- Minimum order size for credit.

- Quantity discount.

Method of payment may be particularly important for export sales. You may need to consider open account, cleared funds, letter of credit, etc.

Do you give settlement discount?

This means that the customer deducts a certain sum or percentage for paying by a certain date. A typical example would be 'Payable after 30 days or 5% settlement for payment within seven days'.

There are obvious advantages and it can be a powerful incentive to get customers to pay promptly. It is often used when money is in short supply and it is worth paying a high price to get the debts paid. Settlement discount is often most effective when first introduced and it can give a kick start to the cash flow. It has to be tightly policed in order to be effective. Unfortunately there are very definite drawbacks:

- Some customers might have paid on time anyway. They get the benefit for nothing.

- It is usually expensive. In the above example 5% is being given for 23 days, which is equal to 79% per year.

- Once introduced it may be difficult to withdraw.

- It requires extra effort to monitor.

- There is always the tendency for the customer to take the discount without paying within the permitted time. There will be difficult decisions and many arguments, both with the customer and within the selling organisation. Customers will cite alleged delivery problems as a reason for paying late and still taking the settlement discount. Sales Directors will shout 'Are you really going to crucify my sales just for six miserable days?'.

Settlement discount is traditional and extremely common in some trades. Customers in these trades may expect it and may even try to take it although it has not been offered. In these circumstances it can be politic to give settlement discount but adjust prices to compensate.

What is a special case and who decides?

In an absolutely fair world all customers would be treated equally but of course life is not really like that. There are normally standard policies that apply to most customers but a few special cases get different treatment. Perhaps a customer is particularly important because of size or prestige. Perhaps a customer is particularly important because of the risk of bad publicity. After all, no one wants to upset Esther Rantzen or Anne Robinson. Perhaps, and let us be honest and recognise the possibility, a customer is important because he is a friend of the Managing Director.

If there are special cases it is as well to recognise the fact and formulate the special policies. Perhaps decisions concerning certain customers should always be referred to a senior level of management.

Policies

Is there a dominant customer and if so what policies are appropriate?

This is an extension of the special case and perhaps it should be called a very special case. It is a customer of vital importance, usually because they take a large part of the sales. Operating with a dominant customer is a not uncommon situation.

There are special dangers in allowing one customer to have a dominant position. Some dominant customers take an unfair advantage almost as a matter of principle. Others do so without thinking about it. Of course it should also be said that many dominant customers are scrupulously fair and do not take any unfair advantages. Nevertheless, you may be very vulnerable to the loss of the business, and you may be in a weak position if a dominant customer does not stick to the agreed terms.

It may be a good idea to try and avoid allowing any one customer to have a dominant position, though this may be easier said than done. For example some defence contractors are almost bound to be in that position. The same is true for many suppliers to companies such as Tesco, Sainsbury's and Marks and Spencer. These retailers are famous for the very detailed demands and quality inspections placed on their suppliers. This is usually for the benefit of all concerned, but especially of themselves.

Some dominant customers ruthlessly exploit their small suppliers by making them wait for payment.

It may be necessary to have special rules for dominant customers and only permit approaches to be made by certain people. If things start to go wrong you should be brutally realistic and consider your options early. If you hold a junior position keep pointing out the risks to the boss. He might not like to hear them but may thank you later.

Overdependence on a dominant customer is one of the biggest causes of business bankruptcies and company liquidations.

Checklist

✓ Do have credit policies. They should be carefully considered with contributions from all concerned, but decisions should be taken at a high level.

✓ Do realise that there will be conflicts of interest with other departments. The credit controller is very important but should not always have everything.

✓ Do aspire to excellence, but be realistic.

✓ Do review credit policies from time to time.

✓ Do ask if you should give credit at all.

✓ Do have a policy for the nominal period of credit and make sure that the customers know it. There are good reasons for making the nominal period of credit as short as possible.

✓ Do have a separate policy for what is in practice acceptable for most of the accounts most of the time.

✓ Do have a policy on sanctions for most of the accounts most of the time.

✓ Do remember that telephone calls are usually the most effective method of collection. Do not forget to consider outside help including credit agencies and factoring.

✓   Do consider whether you should insure some or all of the debts.

✓   Do make your conditions of sale legally effective. This is important and frequently mishandled.

✓   Do consider, at least briefly, the other policies in this chapter.

✓   Do be careful if you have special cases and even more so if you have a dominant customer. If there are problems you should acknowledge them quickly, then face up to the implications.

chapter four

Opening a new account

Introduction

The actions that you take, or do not take, when opening a new account will send a signal to your new customer. If you take no action at all then the customer will receive a very definite signal, though not one that it is in your interest to send. A company that acts in a business-like way, and continues to do so when the first invoices become due for payment, is laying the foundations for satisfactory future trading.

Most customers will respect a business-like approach and will respond in a similar manner. In many cases it will improve the relationship. Of course, sometimes this will not appear to happen. Customers may respond in an angry manner, or a pained manner, or they may ignore your requests for information and acknowledgments. It may be hard to see at the time, but this represents a success for credit control and your procedures, assuming of course that you really are acting in a responsible way.

If there are going to be problems it is much better to know about them at the beginning and to confront them straight away. They do not get easier through being left until after some damage has been done. Also, it is generally easier to get things put right before trading has started and a pattern has been formed.

If you take no action when an account is opened, you are in practice agreeing to the customer's terms including the customer's payment terms. This may well be the legal effect as well as the practical effect. You are very probably committing yourself to a problem if you want to dispute the customer's terms later. You are also taking a calculated risk (or probably an uncalculated risk) about the possibility of incurring a bad debt.

It is worth emphasising three things that the seller should achieve when an account is opened:

- The customer should know and accept the main terms of trading. Most especially, the customer should know and accept the agreed period of credit. This acceptance should be legally effective as well as morally effective.

- The seller should have all the factual information needed to identify the customer, run the account properly and give good service.

- The seller should have sufficient information to be satisfied as to the customer's credit standing. If not, the seller should be able to obtain the information by taking references or by some other means.

Application for a credit account

It may be possible to achieve all the above by means of an exchange of letters or in some other way. However, it is very often good practice to ask the customer to fill in a form asking for a credit account. This is particularly true when the prospective customer is relatively small or relatively unknown. It is very suitable indeed when members of the public are asking for credit.

No one form can encompass all the special circumstances and possibilities. You should design one that suits your own needs. The following is a good all-purpose example. You may find it helpful to study it, then see if it should be altered to meet your own requirements.

Example of a good application form for a credit account

To: **J Perkins Ltd**
14 King Street
Hertford

Dear Sir

We request you to open a credit account in the name of:

_____

Address _____

_____

We accept that all invoices are payable within 30 days of date of issue. We have read your standard conditions of sale and agree that they will govern all trading between us. The maximum amount of credit required is expected to be £_____

Details of two trade referees are given below and we authorise you to make the normal enquiries of them.

Signature_____

Name_____

Position_____

Referee 1

Name_____

Address_____

_____

_____

Referee 2

Name_____

Address_____

_____

_____

This form achieves quite a lot. For a start it gives the exact name and address of the buyer, which will be needed for several business purposes. It should disclose whether or not the buyer is a company which will be vital information if legal action is ever taken. It is quite common for initial information on name and address to be not quite right. This is an opportunity to get it perfect. Apart from anything else it looks bad if a computer issues, probably for years on end, invoices and statements containing the same mistakes.

The form requires signature and the signer's name and position are also requested. It may be useful to have a name in the records in case contact has to be made. It also makes psychological sense. At least one person working for the buyer is more likely to take things seriously if they have put their signature on the form.

Very importantly the form includes the phrase '*We accept that all invoices are payable within 30 days of date of issue*'. This is probably the most important sentence in the entire form. It is absolutely clear and unambiguous. The buyer cannot say that he did not agree and it is a legal as well as a moral obligation. It will be part of the general conditions of sale but it is so important that it is flagged separately. The general conditions will probably not be read and this probably does not matter, but the period of payment does matter. The buyer must know it.

Conditions of sale are covered in Chapter 15. In that chapter it is explained that the seller's conditions of sale very often do not govern the contract. This is not necessarily because there is anything wrong with them. It is because they have not been agreed by the buyer at the time that the contract is made. This form overcomes the problem. It requires a signature and it states that the terms will apply to all trading; not just the first order.

In practice many buyers will happily sign the form without having read the standard conditions of sale or even having seen them. This is very silly of them as sellers' standard conditions are frequently unfair and load the dice against the buyer.

However, this is the buyer's problem. This Guide contains credit control advice for sellers. If you ever read a handbook for buyers it will quite rightly tell you to study the terms carefully and strike out any clauses that you do not like. Needless to say, as a seller, you should have supplied a copy of the standard terms or be willing to do so if asked.

One final point on conditions of sale should be made. The person signing should have *ostensible authority* to do so. This means that it is reasonable to think that he or she can commit the buyer. It is not a problem in the overwhelming majority of cases. But to take it to absurd extremes, an office cleaner should not sign the form if the purchase relates to a nuclear power station. In these circumstances the buyer would not be legally committed.

The form specifies the maximum amount of credit likely to be required. This may be of great interest to the sales department. The main purpose though, is to help decide what level of checks are required. If, for example, the buyer specifies £70 it may be cost-effective to put on a credit limit of £100 and take no further action. If action is necessary it will influence the number of references taken and their interpretation. It may influence the decision whether or not to get a report from a credit reference agency.

The form requires two trade references to be given. Trade references are discussed more fully later in this chapter.

As stated earlier, you should probably design a form to suit your own particular needs. Do remember public relations considerations. The form should be well laid out, printed on good quality paper and easy to fill in. A very common fault is to make the lines too close together with insufficient space for the answers. This makes it less likely that you will get the right information. The following are some of the points not included in the example, but which you might want to consider:

- A contact name in the accounts office.

- Bank details for the purposes of a bank reference.

- Address of company registered office and company registration number.

The last point helps identify a company for the purpose of status checks, helps obtain copies of accounts from Companies House, and is required information if legal action is ever taken. It is a rather intimidating requirement and not usually included. It does possibly risk offending the customer but conveys the message that you take credit seriously. It is more commonly required for big orders.

You will probably have seen a lot of badly designed credit application forms. The whole subject is important for the image of the organisation and a good job can help that image. On the other hand a bad job can be a public relations disaster and a personal experience illustrates the point.

After several times paying cash for my car servicing and repairs, I applied for a credit account at a major garage. The credit application form looked like a poor photocopy of an original 1950s designed form. I completed it and confidently awaited confirmation of credit approval. 24 hours later I received a blunt two line letter telling me that my application for credit was refused. The letter was signed by the Managing Director and no reason was given.

I was both annoyed and alarmed. I am punctilious about paying my bills and I am a writer on credit control. It is not a good recommendation to be turned down for credit. So I rang the Managing Director and asked if he was willing to give me the reason. He replied that it was policy to only give credit to trade accounts or to private customers who had bought a car directly from them. It seemed a very sensible policy and one that I was happy to accept. But the handling of it was a public relations disaster.

Trade references

A certain amount of cynicism about trade references may be permitted. This is because a company in difficulties may make prompt payments to two or three suppliers in order to maintain a supply of good references. There is also the possibility of fraud such as a customer writing his own from an accommodation address. My wife once worked for a company that was deceived in this way, but at least the swindlers had a sense of humour. They called their fraudulent enterprise 'Conns'.

Despite this, surprisingly few customers do indulge in these practices and useful information will very often be obtained. Taking trade references is much more common than a few years ago and reflects the increasing professionalisation of credit control.

Giving a trade reference is an unproductive chore for the person nominated. It is only fair, as well as being in your interest, to make it as easy as possible. You should send a reply paid envelope and a letter or form that can be marked and returned in a minute or so. If you ask for an individually typed letter you are much less likely to get a reply. It is best to ask definite questions and to mention a specific sum for credit. A referee may in good faith give a glowing opinion based on his experience of giving £100 credit. This is all to the good but perhaps you had £20,000 in mind.

A distressingly large number of people seek references then disregard an unsatisfactory reply. If you are going to do this you may as well save your time and the cost of the two postage stamps. If a reference is unsatisfactory do not proceed without some firm assurance from another source. If necessary seek further references from your customer and seek out information from elsewhere. Perhaps a tight credit limit is appropriate, coupled with close management vigilance. You may of course very occasionally receive a rogue, misleading reference. It could be malicious but more likely it will be based on a misunderstanding of the questions.

Equally important, you should not ignore the failure to give a response. This is even more common. Some potential referees may not respond because they are afraid of libel, or because they do not want to let down an existing customer who may be a friend. Also, of course, they may not reply because they are too busy, or lazy, or have lost the form. A few may have a policy of not giving references. Whatever the reason, no news is most definitely not good news. You should never ignore the lack of a reply.

It is worth trying a telephone call. Often the referee will be willing to say something that he would not put in writing. If he has lost the form, or just not got round to it, a telephone call will usually solve the problem. Even if no information is forthcoming it is often possible to make a deduction from the tone of voice used. You may get something like 'Oh they're OK – but it's head office policy not to give references'. He just has.

The Department of Trade and Industry advises in its booklet *Make The Cash Flow* that you should use only referees selected by yourself not the customer. This is obviously preferable but it may be difficult to get the right names and addresses.

There are many different forms for requesting a reference and requirements vary. The following is a good all-purpose example.

Example of a good request for a trade reference

PRIVATE AND CONFIDENTIAL

Dear Sir

J R Smith Ltd of 2, Chiltern Street, Luton

The above has given your name as a trade reference. We would be grateful if you would answer the questions at the foot of this letter and return it in the enclosed prepaid envelope.

Your reply will be treated in strict confidence and at any time we will be pleased to respond to a similar request from yourselves.

Yours faithfully

W Brown
Credit Controller

How long has the above named traded with you?_____

What is the highest credit allowed? £ _____

What are your payment terms?_____

Is payment normally Prompt/Slow/Very Slow

Do you recommend them for total credit of £ _____ Yes/No

Any other information that you think might be helpful.

_____

_____

_____

Bank references

Many customers will only have an account with one bank. This in an advantage because this one bank must be used and the customer will not be able to select the one most likely to give a favourable opinion. A bank reference will only be given without responsibility by the issuing bank.

Until recently banks would only reply to another bank. Fortunately, practice has now changed and they will respond directly, but only if they are in receipt of their customer's written authority to give an opinion. It is normal to obtain the customer's consent on a standard form and to forward it to the bank with the enquiry. Banks make a charge for giving a reference. In most cases this will be between £8 and £11 but in some cases it may be up to £25.

A bank will only give an opinion based on information available. It will give its opinion of the soundness and safety of its customer. It will not comment on how quickly or slowly, it pays its bills, which is one of the things you would most like to know. Banks will not lie but they will probably not want to damn their customers. This should be remembered. Bank responses are likely to be couched in time-honoured terms which need interpretation.

Favourable phrases include:

- 'Undoubted' (this is the best reply of all).

- 'Considered good for your figures.'

Unfavourable phrases include:

- 'We are unable to speak for your figures' (this is the worst reply of all).

- 'Fully committed.'

You may get a reply like:

- 'The figure is higher than we are accustomed to seeing. However, the customer is a client of long standing and we do not think that he would enter into a commitment that he could not see his way clear to fulfil.'

This is a warning but the bank has good experience with the customer.

There is usually not much point in seeking a reference for a soundly constructed major public company. This is because you will be told that it is a soundly constructed major public company. You already have that information and really need to know if they pay their bills promptly. Bank references are useful for avoiding bad debts but not much good for avoiding slow payers.

Credit limits

When you have completed all the checks that you consider necessary, and opened an account, your new customer is licensed to take deliveries and expose you to risk. The same is true if you have not carried out any checks at all. Trading to a credit limit is a way of limiting that risk and it may be done for one of two reasons:

1. In view of the customer's modest requirements only limited checks have been done, or possibly no checks at all. There is a limit to how much time and money it is sensible to spend. A credit limit caps the exposure and may be a reasonable compromise.

2. The checks reveal cause for concern. Depending on the circumstances you may decide to take the risk, after all profits are made from business that you accept, not from orders that you turn down. However, it may be sensible to limit the risk by setting an upper limit to the exposure.

You may not want to tell the customer that you have a limit and what it is. You may therefore not do so, particularly if the reason is that you have only run limited checks. If he wants to increase the level of business you can run the checks quickly and increase the limit. The customer need never know.

On the other hand, there are often good reasons for telling the customer of the limit, particularly if the reason is concern about the customer's standing. He will need to know anyway if it results in supplies being restricted. It is only fair and gives the customer a chance to put his case. Perhaps fresh references can be supplied, or perhaps a credit reference agency is still holding out-of-date information.

There is a further reason for using credit limits. They can cap losses from fraud or due to a sudden worsening in the fortunes of a customer. Take for example a customer asking for £4,000 credit. Your checks show that this seems reasonable and you open an account with a limit of say £5,000. Then let us suppose the customer places an order for £20,000. It may be excellent business, but it may be part of a fraud, or it may be because the customer cannot get credit elsewhere.

Without the £5,000 limit the order may well have been fulfilled. After all it is an existing account and perhaps nothing is overdue for payment. You can run further checks and review the limit, but in the meantime your loss cannot exceed £5,000.

Needless to say, credit limits are not necessarily set for all time. They can be reviewed. The act of reviewing a credit limit forces management to make an active decision. Even if the decision is to take a big risk it is a conscious decision made after reviewing the facts.

Checklist

✓ Do do something when a new account is opened. The absolute minimum is to write and confirm the main terms.

✓ Do remember that to do nothing probably commits you in practice (and perhaps legally as well) to the customer's terms.

✓ Do remember that the best time to sort out a problem is right at the start. It does not get easier.

✓ Do make sure that the customer knows and accepts the period of credit.

✓ Do make sure that you have all the factual information that you need.

✓ Do get all the information that you need to make a reasonable assessment of the credit risk. The bigger the proposed debt the higher should be the standard of information that you seek.

✓ Do consider an 'Application For Credit' form. Design a good one using the advice in this chapter.

✓ Do consider obtaining trade references. They are often very useful. Do not ignore a bad reply and do not ignore a failure to reply. If necessary, follow up with a telephone call.

✓ Do remember that a bank reference may tell you about the safety of a debt. It is not likely to tell you if you will be paid promptly.

✓ Do seriously consider credit limits. They are often very useful. Detailed advice is in this chapter.

chapter five

Effective paperwork

Introduction

The politician Iain Macleod told the story of his asking for directions in a foreign city. He received the reply 'If I was going there, I wouldn't be starting from here'. That might seem witty but not very relevant to credit control, but there is a point and a connection. The point is that if you get the foundations right, later chasing may be easier and perhaps unnecessary. It is best to start in the right place.

Effective paperwork is one of the basic foundations of effective credit control. Different types of paperwork are considered later in the chapter but they should all incorporate the following four key features:

- It should be of good quality.

- It should be well-presented.

- It should be accurate.

- It should be timely.

It is generally a mistake to skimp on the physical quality of the paperwork. You do not have to spend a fortune, but it is a mistake to let it fall below a certain standard. My personal opinion (not universally shared) is that it pays to aim well above that standard. This is particularly true if your business is any way associated with communication (such as public relations), or if your invoicing is a relatively low number of high value items.

Well-presented means that it should be logically laid out and contain all the required information, but no more. It is usually a mistake to make invoices, statements, etc, double as advertisements. You usually get poor invoices or statements coupled with an ineffective advertisement. You might even annoy the customers.

Accurate and timely are both self-explanatory words. It is very easy to underestimate the importance of timeliness. It is often better to produce a document that is 95% complete (but not of course inaccurate), and right on time, than to delay it for the sake of the final 5%.

You will very probably agree with all the above but do not move on without taking an objective look and seeing what happens in your own organisation.

An objective look

It is very likely that you have become so used to the designs of your invoices and statements that you do not see them objectively. Because you are 100% familiar with them you consider, perhaps wrongly, that they are ideal for your customers.

An entertaining experiment will illustrate the truth of this. Ask a friend to put both hands behind his or her back, then ask your friend to describe in detail the face of his or her watch. What colour is it? Are there 12 numbers or are there a series of marks? Or are there a mixture of marks and numbers? Are there roman numerals? If there are marks, how many and are they all the same size?

Your friend will almost certainly not get it exactly right and quite possibly will get it horrendously wrong. Yet he or she will have glanced at the watch face at least 40 times a day, probably every day for years on end.

Invoices, statements and other forms are rather like that. You see them frequently but perhaps do not really know them. Put yourself in the customer's shoes and have an objective look.

Do they look impressive? Are they good for the image of the company? Do they demand to go on top of the pile rather than on the bottom? Do they give your customers all the information that they want, such as order numbers, delivery addresses, and so on? Are they well printed on good quality paper?

It can be useful to ask friends for their opinions. Seal an invoice in an envelope then imagine that you are a customer opening the envelope.

See what happens in your own organisation

Try spending a few minutes in the Bought Ledger Department of your own company or organisation. Try to be inconspicuous and just watch what happens. This is especially valuable if it is a busy department with a lot of invoices and statements. See which ones the staff deal with first and ask them why. They might not know the reasons themselves but they will be following subconscious rules. What happens in your own Bought Ledger Department probably happens in the Bought Ledger Departments of your customers. You may learn some useful lessons.

All documents are important, but we will consider in detail invoices, statements and orders. Invoices are possibly the most important so these are considered first.

Invoices

Timing of invoices

It is worth going to a lot of trouble to see that invoices are posted as promptly as possible. In many cases they will be launched into a bureaucracy that takes several weeks to approve invoices for payment. The approved invoice will then be passed to an accounts office that may take a week or more to post it to the account.

The same accounts office may make payments on fixed dates, perhaps only once a month. Let us consider the following not wholly unusual example:

- Royal Mail takes two days to deliver the invoice (no criticism is implied – second class postage is assumed).

- The customer takes 21 days to approve the invoice for payment.

- The customer's Bought Ledger Department takes seven days to post the invoice to the account.

- The customer pays accounts only on the fifth day of each month.

An invoice posted second class on April 6th will be posted to the account on May 6th, too late for inclusion in the cheque run. It is monstrously unfair, but you may have to wait until 5th June for the cheque. On the other hand, an invoice posted first class on April 4th will be posted to the account on May 3rd. You should get paid a month earlier.

It is a general rule of credit control that it pays to start early and this applies to sending out invoices. For very large invoices with short payment terms it may even be worth considering hand delivery or messenger delivery. If credit is costing £300 per day then £30 for motorbike delivery may be good value. Do not overlook the possibility of sending an invoice by fax or e-mail, with a hard copy to follow.

Dating of invoices

You should normally date an invoice on the earliest date contractually possible. This is normally, but not always, the date of delivery. There is no requirement, legal or otherwise, for an invoice to be dated the day that it is produced and posted (which in any case may be different dates). This is so important that it is worth repeating.

- An invoice should normally be dated the first date that is contractually possible.

The contract may permit stage payments or the invoicing of installments. If so, you should take advantage of it. Many customers have payment systems geared to calendar months, such as 'net monthly account'. This means that all invoices are due at the end of the month following invoice date. It may not be fair and it may not be your terms, but it is what the customer will try to do. This means that the customer will say that an invoice dated April 1st is not due for payment until May 31st (of course he might actually pay it much later). On the other hand an invoice dated March 31st would be regarded as due on April 30th, a whole month earlier.

VAT law requires a VAT invoice to be dated not more than 14 days after the event that causes it. This is normally delivery, but may be some other contractual event, such as completion of a specification.

Size and frequency of invoices

It is usually better to send small invoices frequently, rather than save up for one big invoice at the end of a series of deliveries. The same applies to stage payments on a contract. Practical advantages are:

- Early invoices will become due for payment more quickly.

- If the customer is short of money he may pay some of the smaller invoices, whereas he would not pay one big invoice for the total.

- A dispute should only hold up payment of one of the invoices, but it might hold up the whole payment if there is just one invoice.

- It may be easier to get the customer's approval on smaller invoices. Larger invoices may require more approval signatures and approval at more senior levels.

My book *Successful Credit Control* published by Hawksmere was first published in 1992. It included the following:

> *The Chief Executive of a major British company has made a rule that no invoices over £50,000 are to be paid without his personal signature on them. Quite apart from any wish to delay payment, it must be remembered that he is an extremely busy man, and he takes holidays. He also travels abroad on business, sometimes for two weeks at a time. This man, who is a household name, will not thank me for giving you the advice, but I am going to anyway. Send him two invoices for £26,000 rather than one for £52,000'.*

I did not feel able to say so at the time, but I was referring to the late Mr Robert Maxwell.

Full details

Never forget that you may be dealing with a bureaucracy. By helping the bureaucrat you may be helping yourself too.

You are asking for trouble if you send an invoice to H.M. Government, Whitehall, London SW1. Similarly, do not address an invoice to Ford Motor Company, Dagenham, Essex. You must give them a lot more help than that. It may eventually reach the right person and it may eventually get paid. But do not bank on it, and certainly do not bank on it being paid quickly. You will do much better if you address the invoice to the right department, preferably with a room number, and mark it for the attention of a named person. Ford will respond best if you:

- Quote the order number.

- Specify the delivery address, which may well be different from the invoice address.

- Only claim what is contractually due.

- Ensure that the invoice adds up correctly and is technically correct.

- Ensure that the invoice is fully legible (some computer-generated multi-part invoices are appalling).

- Quote a named person if this is relevant.

Very often the order number is the critical factor. So you need to ensure that your system records order numbers and quotes them on invoices. This can be very difficult at times. The person actually placing the order may not share the enthusiasm for order numbers and may say that it does not matter or will be supplied later. This is often the case when goods are wanted urgently, (this is a general point – not specifically aimed at Ford). But be aware of the problem. It is usually a good idea to put the standard conditions of sale on the back of the invoice.

Statements

Some suppliers do not send statements. They rely on customers to pay on invoice only, or failing that, in response to collection procedures. They justify this by saying that it saves money, and also by saying that some customers completely ignore statements and rely entirely on their own records.

This is quite true; some statements go straight into the bin. Nevertheless it is, in my view, usually a false economy not to send statements. It is worth doing for the sake of customers that do use them. They help customers reconcile accounts, ask for copies of missing invoices, and so on. There are also audit and control advantages in sending statements. Many frauds have been discovered because a customer queried a puzzling item on a statement.

Some companies only pay on statement and will not pay on invoice until they are asked. This is extremely unfair but it pays to accept reality.

Good practice for statements is very similar to good practice for invoices, namely:

- Post them as soon as possible after the month end, within the first day if possible.

- Payment terms should be boldly stated.

- It should be very clear what is owing, how much is overdue and when the remainder becomes due.

- They should look impressive, be logically laid out and give all the information that the customer will need.

- It is usually a good idea to put the standard conditions of sale on the back.

You may face the age-old dilemma concerning the need to delay statements in order to include all relevant information. In some systems it can take several days to get the last invoices raised, cash allocated and queries resolved. This is particularly true when there are a lot of invoices. It is, after all, good practice to send out up-to-date, fully accurate statements. If you have this problem you should:

- Look at your systems again. Is it really true that things cannot be speeded up? Perhaps you are dependant on your colleagues in other departments. If so, try really hard to be persuasive, or involve a higher level of management.

- Decide exactly how you are going to strike the compromise between speed and completeness. Individual circumstances alter cases, but perhaps you should come down more on the side of speed. This is particularly true when your terms specify a short payment period.

Order forms

It is likely that the order form will be the key document in determining what terms legally govern the contract. This is covered in detail in Chapter 15. What happens afterwards is interesting but does not normally affect the conditions. What matters is what is agreed (or at least stated) when the contract is made.

It is usual to have the standard conditions of sale on the back of the order form, but with a prominent statement on the front pointing out that they are printed on the back. If this is not done there is a risk that the terms might not be legally effective. The exception is the terms for payment, which should be prominently printed on the front. The customer should be well aware of the commitment that is being made.

Depending on individual circumstances, it is usual to make the order part of a carbonated set. One copy of the order is left with the customer, or a copy is returned to him after acceptance by the seller.

Needless to say, the order form should be well laid-out, easy to read, printed on reasonable quality paper, etc.

Checklist

✓ Do ensure that documents are well printed on paper of a reasonable standard.

✓ Do ensure that documents are well laid out, and contain all the necessary information.

✓ Do ensure that all documents are fully accurate.

✓ Do ensure that all documents are submitted promptly.

✓ Do look very critically at the paperwork issued by your own organisation. Self-delusion is a common mistake.

✓ Do normally date invoices on the first date permitted by contract. Do this even if they are not produced and posted until later.It may make a big difference to the payment date.

✓ Do remember that it is often better to send several small invoices rather than one big one. This is especially true if some of the invoices can carry an earlier date.

✓ Do send statements (in nearly all cases).

✓ Do send out statements promptly. It may be better to send them on time but not quite complete, rather than to delay posting.

✓ Do remember that an order form is a key legal document.

✓ Do ensure that orders, invoices and statements, all state prominently what is the expected payment period or date.

chapter six

Letters

Introduction

Many people believe that effective letter writing is a dying art. If this is true, part of the reason must be that word processors, and other technological marvels, have made it very easy to quickly produce vast numbers of standardised letters. Standard letters and individually composed letters do have some common features, but the differences make them worth considering separately.

Standard letters

Standard letters are considered to be among the less effective collection methods. Nevertheless, they are bound to form an essential part of collection procedures for many suppliers. Economic factors dictate this, especially when there are a large number of small debts to be collected. Telephone calls are a particularly effective form of collection and they often work best when integrated with a system of standard letters. Perhaps a telephone call should come after a standard letter, and before the final warning letter.

Let us start by acknowledging that a certain number of standard letters will go straight into the bin. This is so, regardless of timing, content, wording and presentation. It is nevertheless worth taking considerable trouble with timing, content, wording and presentation. This is because it will improve the response of customers who are willing to act on a request made in a standard letter.

One of the disadvantages of a standard letter is that there is no immediate contact with the recipient. You cannot look him in the eye as you can on a personal visit, and you cannot ask a follow-up question as you can with a telephone call.

A compensating advantage is that it suits some buyers, particularly the bigger buyers, to have a piece of paper. It is the bureaucrats again, as mentioned in the last chapter. The arguments are similar to those for sending statements.

Whatever the system of standard letters, it pays to vary the content and timing occasionally. This is because customers get used to them and get to know for how long they can safely be ignored. Some customers will take advantage of this. If your system culminates in a final warning letter on say day 58, some customers will plan to always pay you on day 62. There is always the risk of this, but you can keep them guessing by changing the wording. Or perhaps go to one letter before the final warning instead of two. This is sound advice for other collection procedures too. Whatever they are, and no matter how good, it is worth slightly varying them from time to time.

Some organisations send out two standard letters before moving to the final warning. A few send more than two, and a tiny misguided minority continue the letters more or less indefinitely. There is a trend towards sending just one letter followed by the final warning letter if necessary. This has a lot to commend it. The customer will have received an invoice, at least one statement (probably more), a standard letter, and will receive a final warning letter before firm action is taken. That should be enough.

Word processors, and other modern equipment, allow high quality standard letters to be prepared with maximum efficiency. They also allow them to be personalised effectively with minimum effort. Good examples are the red reminder letters issued by British Telecom and the Utilities. Everyone knows that they are standard letters but they are efficient and they work. Of course, it helps that everyone genuinely fears the ultimate sanction. No one wants their telephone cut off, or their water supply terminated.

Good standard letters incorporate the following points:

- As with invoices and statements, they should look impressive.

- They should be short.

- The first letter should be sent immediately the debt is due, or very shortly afterwards. Remember, the earlier you start, the earlier you are likely to be paid.

- The tone should always be polite but firm. You are entitled to ask for payment and should never apologise for doing so (unless you have got your facts wrong of course).

- Give the customer an opportunity to raise queries. As well as being good for customer relations you want to know what the queries are.

- Letters should nearly always be individually signed. Mass mailings, such as those by British Telecom, are a legitimate exception.

- You should ensure that your letter looks individually prepared, even if it is not. Do not duplicate or photo-copy letters.

- The wording of a second or subsequent letter should always disclose that it is a second or subsequent letter. It will lose some of its impact if the recipient thinks that it is a first letter.

- If possible, letters should be addressed to a named person. If you do not have a name use a title such as 'Chief Accountant'.

- Do not use a phrase such as 'Please ignore this letter if payment has been made within the last seven days'. It looks weak and you can safely rely on the customer to ignore it in these circumstances. You should know if you have received the money, and if you have not you are entitled to ask, even if it is actually on the way.

As stated earlier, the appropriate number of letters will vary according to circumstances, and so will the precise wording. The following are two examples of good all-purpose first and second standard letters. Note that they are short but make the point. The intervals between letters are for you to decide. The letters are examples, not an endorsement of a particular time gap.

Example of a good first standard letter

J Jones Esq
Chief Accountant
Burns and Fish Ltd
38 Broad Street
Northampton

1 October 1998

Dear Mr Jones

We notice that a balance of £269.24 is overdue for payment. We are not aware of any reason why payment should not be made but please do let me have details if this is the case.

If your payment is on the way to us please accept our thanks. Otherwise could we please have your remittance by return.

Yours sincerely

K Green
Credit Controller

Example of a good second standard letter

J Jones Esq
Chief Accountant
Burns and Fish Ltd
38 Broad Street
Northampton

10 October 1998

Dear Mr Jones

We cannot trace a reply to our letter of 1 October requesting payment of the overdue balance of £269.24.

If there is any reason why payment should not be made would you let us know by return. Otherwise as the account is now very overdue we must ask for immediate settlement.

Yours sincerely

K Green
Credit Controller

The final warning letter

The final warning letter is the last step before handing the debt over to the legal process. As such, it is also covered in Chapter 16 which deals with work preparatory to legal action. The final warning letter may be the concluding standard letter in a series of standard letters. It is, though, also issued in other circumstances.

In some cases all attempts to get payment will fail. You must then either give up or take steps to enforce payment. This nearly always means legal action but a believable final warning will often secure the money. Unfortunately, some people will cynically delay payment until the last possible minute. A credible final warning letter is getting very close to something that the great majority of debtors do not want to face.

As a final warning often works, and because it can retain a customer where legal action would not, it is best to issue such a letter before commencing legal proceedings. The letter should have the following features:

- By definition there is only one final warning letter. If you send more than one, something is wrong with your system.

- Do not make empty threats. If you do not mean it, do not say it.

- Make it short and to the point.

- Despite the purpose, make it polite and firm, not abusive.

- State the exact deadline and the amount to be paid. It is better to specify an exact date rather than a number of elapsed days. You should use a phrase such as 'unless payment of £800 has been received by February 17th'.

- State exactly what will happen if payment is not made by the specified date. Do not use vague phrases such as 'other steps' or 'we will be forced to place the matter in other hands'.

In order to achieve maximum impact it is a good idea to send the final warning by recorded delivery. This does not imply lack of faith in Royal Mail and you would not normally have to prove that the letter was delivered. The reason is purely psychological. It concentrates the mind of the recipient to see the yellow sticker on the envelope. He or she will think that it is important, which it is.

For the same reason it is often a good idea to address the final warning letter to a different person, with a copy to the person you have dealt with so far. If the debtor is a company it is sound to address the letter to the Company Secretary. The prospect of legal action will be bad news for the Company Secretary, not least because it will involve work and expense. He may therefore put pressure on his colleagues. Also, the person actually holding up the payment may not welcome the Company Secretary's involvement, and may as a result take steps to keep him away.

The following is a good example of a final warning letter. It is the third and final standard letter of the set. The first two are earlier in this chapter.

Example of a good final warning letter

The Company Secretary
Burns and Fish Ltd
38 Broad Street
Northampton

20 October 1998

Dear Sir

Overdue Balance of £269.24

We notice with regret the above balance is still outstanding. Although we wrote on 1 October and 10 October we have received neither payment nor a reason why payment should not be made.

We must now tell you that we expect payment to be made by 27 October. If payment has not been received by that date we will pass the matter to our solicitors with instructions to commence legal proceedings. This will be done without further warning to you.

Yours faithfully

K Green
Credit Controller

cc Mr J Jones

Individually composed letters

An individually prepared letter is expensive and time consuming to produce. In many ways it is less likely to be as effective as a telephone call. Before letters are lightly dismissed, however, please consider the following advantages:

- It is a permanent record. A telephone call may be forgotten but a letter (unless it is thrown away by the recipient) is a permanent reminder.

- It is an opportunity to convey complicated information. A telephone call may just get over the message 'You owe a lot of money – please do something about it'. Admittedly this is an excellent message to convey. A letter can list the invoices making up the total, detail progress in resolving disputes, and so on. It is good for sorting out a complicated account, as opposed to getting most of it paid, but not necessarily all of it.

- A letter can be less humiliating for the recipient. I used to be responsible for policing settlement discount and from time to time had to disallow it because payment was too late. I always conveyed the bad news by letter, and only telephoned if a further payment did not arrive in a reasonable time. Disallowing settlement discount almost always results in anger or humiliation, or probably both.

- A well-written letter can be a pleasure to receive (even if money is owing) and it can enhance customer relations.

Much advice for individually composed letters is similar to the advice for standard letters. They should be as short as possible, consistent with achieving their objectives. Normally they should be friendly and personal, especially if you know the person to whom it is being sent.

It is even more important that you get the facts right. One of the advantages of a letter is that it is a permanent record. The last thing that you want is a permanent record of a mistake. Needless to say the letter should be well-composed, well-produced and be grammatically correct.

A light touch and humour can be particularly effective, especially if you know the addressee. Perhaps you could start with a sentence such as 'It is part of my mission statement to sort out your account'. You will probably be able to think of examples that suit your personality and style.

Checklist

✓   Do consider standard letters if you have a large number of small debts.

✓   Do consider a system that integrates telephone calls with standard letters. This is especially effective.

✓   Do occasionally vary the content and timing of standard letters.

✓   Do personalise standard letters.

✓   Do make all letters look physically impressive.

✓   Do make all letters as short as possible. Long letters may not get read.

✓   Do make the tone of all letters 'polite but firm'.

✓   Do give an opportunity to raise queries.

✓   Do send the first letter at an early date. The sooner you ask, the sooner you are likely to be paid.

✓   If it is a second or subsequent letter, do state that it is a second or subsequent letter.

✓   Do try to address the letter to a named person.

✓   Do send only one final warning letter. It is a contradiction of terms to send more than one.

✓   Do not make empty threats. If you do not mean it, do not say it.

✓   Do ensure that the final warning letter spells out the exact consequences. There should be no ambiguity.

7
chapter seven

Collection by telephone

Introduction

Telephoning is one of the most effective methods of collection, probably second only to personal visits. It is normally much more successful than letters, although letters do have the advantages that were detailed in the last chapter. Telephone calls are particularly effective when used in conjunction with standard letters.

Readers below a certain age will find it hard to credit but, until comparatively recently, telephone calls were expensive. Business calls were commonly put off until the afternoon when they were cheaper. Those days have now gone. Telephoning is cheap and it is getting cheaper, both in relative terms and some years in absolute terms. It is virtually never sensible not to use the telephone because of the costs (long foreign calls may be an exception).

Unfortunately, use of the telephone is still a heavy user of time. Even this is not so true as it was. Telephone technology has made it easier to make more calls in a given period. As calls are easier and cheaper to make, more calls get made. Regrettably (from the caller's viewpoint), this is leading to more people using technology to protect themselves from unwanted calls, and to put the receiver in charge of the situation. It is getting more and more common to have to listen to recorded music and recorded messages. Even worse is the recorded message followed by an invitation to push a button according to the purpose of the call. All too often this finishes up in the wrong place or nowhere at all.

A telephone caller may be able to make 15 or so calls in an hour, though may not be able to keep this rate up for hour after hour. If the debts are complicated, and he has to prepare for the calls and answer queries, his progress will be much slower. If there are only a few accounts it may be possible to start at A and work through to Z. For most of us a system of priorities is highly desirable. Examples of such systems are:

1. Largest amounts first.

2. Most overdue first.

3. Most likely to respond asked first.

4. Most worrying first.

Some of the above points are contradictory. It is up to you to set your own priorities. If you are worried about bad debts you should go for points 2 and 4. If you want a quick flow of cash you should go for points 1 and 3.

The right psychology

Many people, perhaps most, dislike telephoning for money. They feel embarrassed and they fear the rudeness that will inevitably be encountered from time to time. If this applies to you, there are five very practical points to help put you in the right frame of mind:

1. You really are 100% morally justified in making the call. If the money was not owing you would not be asking for it. Deep down you know this is true, so keep reminding yourself. There is no need to be embarrassed. If anyone is rude to you, that says something about them, not about you. If you were at fault the customer would quite rightly ring you. So you are quite right to ring the customer when payment is late. **It's true – remember it.**

2. You might feel that your telephone skills are not as good as you would wish. Even if this is true, you should console yourself with the knowledge that sheer effort has a tremendous influence on the results achieved. The mere act of asking does persuade a substantial number of customers to pay.

   Perhaps experience shows that 60% of customers send a cheque within a week of being asked. If you make 100 calls, 60 cheques will arrive. But if you can squeeze in 110 calls, then 66 cheques will arrive.

So remember the slogan *Ask Early, Ask Often*. Keep reminding yourself that you are achieving results.

3. Sometimes a telephone call achieves results despite appearing to be a failure at the time. Sometimes it jogs someone's memory, or they have a policy of only paying when asked. So tell yourself, even when you get a bad reaction, that you probably have not been wasting your time.

4. The way you perform can be influenced by the way that you feel. There may well be things that you can do to improve the way that you feel. If so do them – only you will know. Many people feel more in charge if they make the call standing up. If it works for them, why not? The customer will never know.

5. Many people find it helpful to say slogans and truisms under their breath when the going gets tough. Examples are '*We are not a bank*' and '*There is no profit until the money is in the bank*'. Other examples were given in Chapter 2. Perhaps you know some better ones.

Preparation for success

This is extremely important and it impacts on the right psychology discussed above. The knowledge that you have thoroughly prepared (if you have) is bound to increase your confidence, and this alone will ensure that the call is more effective.

A badly prepared call may do more harm than good. So do the preparation thoroughly. However, do not fall into the trap of preparing so much that there is not enough time to make the calls. It can be a fine line and you have to strike a balance.

Ideally, you should have at your fingertips:

- The total amount of the debt.

- The amount that is overdue.

- The dates and amounts of the invoices making up the debt.

- Details of any outstanding disputes.

- Knowledge of the history of the account.

- Details of any promises made but not kept. You should be able to quote names, dates and amounts promised.

This is a formidable list and it may not be practical in every case. A balance has to be struck.

The telephone call

The right tone to use

It pays to adopt a friendly attitude most of the time, and certainly at the start of the call. Most people (but by no means all) will respond best to this approach. If you call the same person regularly you might even establish a telephone friendship. This is good for business as the other person may be reluctant to let down a friend.

Your tone should be firm as well as friendly. This is not a contradiction. You will almost certainly know several well-liked and respected people whose attitude and voice are both firm and friendly. They are liked, but people sense that they mean what they say and should not be trifled with. This is what you should aim for.

As well as firmness, your voice should reflect efficiency and confidence. This is easy advice to give, but it should develop with practice and if you work at it. Confidence will come more easily if you know that you have prepared well and are doing a good job. If this is not the case, try and sound confident anyway.

Try to treat people as individuals and to treat each call individually. This may not be easy when you are working down a long list of names with little to differentiate one from another. But nevertheless, try. It is easier if you know the people, or if different features of the account make them stand out.

Best of all, engage people in a genuine conversation. This does mean treating people as individuals and it means genuinely listening to what is said. It does not necessarily mean agreeing with them, but it means listening and considering the possibility that they may have a point.

People respond badly to a voice that sounds as though it is reading from a script, and is doing so for the tenth time that morning. They tend to react from their own script, which may be to say that they will look into it. All too often the matter is then forgotten. So, you must make your call sound different, interesting, friendly and firm, You must also make it a two-way conversation, not a one-way monologue.

Dealing with rudeness

There is a well known piece of advice about 'letting the air out of the balloon'. If someone feels very strongly about something it is usually best to let him have his say. He will probably not be willing to listen to your point of view until he has got it off his chest. This most definitely does not mean agreeing with him or letting him walk all over you; it means letting him make his point.

When the point has been made, consider whether there is any justification in it. It may be hard to be objective in these circumstances, but try. If he is right, say something like 'I am sorry you felt that you had to put it like that, but you are quite right. I'll get it seen to'.

Sometimes you will find that the customer has got a point but that it is only part of what is at issue. Admit the point, but do not be deterred from asking for the rest to be paid. This is a very common failing. If one invoice is in dispute, isolate it and ask for the rest to be paid. If there is a problem with a large invoice say that you will sort it out, but ask for a realistic payment on account.

If the customer is wrong tell him so in the best way that you can. This means putting your point fairly and constructively, but also firmly and politely. The best outcome is that you will persuade him that you are right. You might even get an apology though that is probably being optimistic. The next best outcome is that you agree to differ, hopefully amicably.

The worst outcome is that you make the point, he does not accept it and is still casting doubts on the marital status of your parents. If this happens you will have to bring the call to an end and consider your next step. Do not mind bringing in someone else on your side and perhaps on his. This is not weakness. The object is to get him to pay, or at least to settle the dispute fairly. If you can get a colleague to do that you will have won.

Getting to the right person

Do not have too many preconceived ideas about who is the right person. The right person is the one who can arrange satisfactory payment. This may be a junior person perhaps even a very junior person. This does not matter so long as the right result is obtained. It is not your job to worry about how the customer organises its internal affairs.

The right person could be the Managing Director but it probably is not, at least not to start with. It is better to make the first approach to a reasonable level of authority, say the Accounts Payable Manager. If you do not get the right result do not hesitate to move to a more senior level.

The above assumes that you are approaching a large organisation. If it is a small organisation it is usually obvious who should be approached. If you know someone in a large organisation it may be a good idea to use that knowledge. It is a very good idea to ask for someone by name.

You may ask, if the customer is a large organisation, which should be approached, the accounts office or the actual buyer. It is usually best to start with the accounts office, then switch to the buyer if necessary. The accounts office may say that they have not got an approved invoice. You then have to speak to the buyer to find out why not. If in doubt speak to both. The slogan *Ask Early, Ask Often* has already been mentioned. Perhaps it should be *Ask Early, Ask Often, Ask Everyone*.

Dealing with a block

Sometimes you will be prevented from speaking to the right person. Either that person will not be available or you will be passed to someone without the authority to help. You may be told that the person is in a meeting. Given the way that so many businesses are run this could well be true.

You may get the response that of course you can speak to Mrs X, but unfortunately she has gone out, or gone to the North Pole via the South Pole. If this happens keep trying, ask for a specific time when she will be there, and ring back.

When dealing with a block be very persistent. Many times you will succeed in the end, if only because the person blocking you will get embarrassed or bored or because someone is locked away doing a job and eventually gets to the end of it. Realistically, however, this will not always be the case. There are switchboard operators and secretaries who will not put you through, no matter what you say and no matter how often you ring. When you have got to the end of the line you must do three things:

- Leave a detailed and unmistakable final message.

- Put it in writing.

- Move on to your sanctions, perhaps a seven day warning letter and a suspension of supplies.

Questions

Using questions effectively

There are two types of question. The first is asked because you do not know the answer and would like to. An example is 'Your cheque was due last Tuesday and it did not come. Can you tell me the reason please?'.

Beware of the customer answering with an excuse or something irrelevant, and if necessary be prepared to lead him firmly back to the point. You may have to say something like 'We did apologise for that and we did give you the extra discount. Can we talk about last month's invoice please? It is two weeks overdue'.

The second type of question is asked when you already know the answer, or think that you do. Questions are often put in a series and it is a technique well known to lawyers who lead witnesses up to a desired admission. The following is an example:

'Did the copy invoice arrive?'

'Has it been approved now?'

'Is your payment run this Friday?'

'Can I expect the cheque on Monday?'

Note how it is done. Each question is a reasonable one and follows on from the one before. It is hard not to say yes to all of them. You may be less likely to get an affirmative answer if you just say 'Can I expect your cheque this Monday?'.

Ask for precise sums

You should be precise and ask for specific sums. The customer may prevaricate and talk about seeing what can be done, or having a look at it. If you have prepared well you will know exactly what is owing so you can be specific.

It may be necessary to press the customer, and ask bluntly why he will not say exactly what will be paid.

The effective conclusion

The best conclusion is a cheque in the post, but whether this is achieved or not you should both know exactly what is going to happen. Perhaps nothing is going to happen, or something is but not exactly what you want. But whatever it is, you should both know. You should try not to end on an inconclusive note.

One of you should say what is going to happen, and if possible it should be the customer who says it. This is because if he has uttered the words he is more likely to feel committed to them. Perhaps a well-timed pregnant pause will prompt him to say them. If you really cannot get him to do it, then ultimately you must do it yourself, perhaps prefaced with some phrase such as 'I am making a note of your promise that …'.

Keep the history

You should prepare for a call and have a certain amount of information in front of you. This will be done more easily if you, or your predecessor, has kept records of previous calls. Similarly, future callers will benefit from records that you now make. Among the details useful to note are:

- Names.

- Times when available.

- Customer's procedures (payment dates, etc).

- Promises given and dates that they were made.

The last point is particularly important and you should be precise. It is OK to say 'You promised me a cheque some time ago'. But it is much better to be able to say 'On 10th April you told me that £3,700 would be sent first class by the end of the week'.

Simple records are usually the best. You should devise a system that gives maximum benefit for minimum work.

Checklist

✓ Do remember that telephoning is one of the most effective collection methods. It is not too costly, but it can be time consuming.

✓ Do telephone according to a list of priorities. It is not usually a good idea to start at A and work through to Z.

✓ Do put yourself in the right frame of mind for telephoning (this chapter tells you how). Remember that there are rewards for effort and remember *Ask Early, Ask Often*.

✓ Do prepare thoroughly for the calls. But do not prepare for so long that there is insufficient time to make enough calls.

✓ Do try to adopt a tone that is both friendly and firm.

✓ Do engage in a genuine conversation and do not sound as through you are reading a script.

✓ Do not be upset by rudeness. It is a reflection on the speaker, not on you.

✓ Do generally speak first to a reasonable level of authority within the accounts department. But do not hesitate to go higher if necessary.

✓ Do be persistent when you are blocked from speaking to the right person. Try and try again. If all else fails leave an unmistakable message, put it in writing, then move on to your sanctions.

✓ Do learn how to use questions effectively.

✓ Do always ask for precise sums.

✓ Do handle the conclusion effectively. You should both know what is going to happen and, ideally, it should be the customer who says it.

✓ Do keep records of your calls. It helps next time.

chapter eight

Overcoming excuses

Introduction

Most credit controllers can tell stories about the implausible excuses given to them. My favourite was being told in 1986 that a purchase ledger was on a computerised system dependent on satellite communications. The Challenger space shuttle had been going to repair a malfunctioning satellite, but due to the tragic accident the purchase ledger information would be unavailable for an indefinite period.

Such stories are funny in retrospect and, let's be fair, perhaps funny at the time. You will of course encounter many more plausible excuses and some of them will be so plausible that they might even be true. Do not overlook the fact that occasionally you might be told the truth, even if it does sound unlikely. Nonetheless, you will be told a lot of lies. This chapter gives much practical advice on how to overcome these excuses.

Like jokes, most of the excuses are variations on just a few themes. An experienced collector will meet the same ones again and again. For convenience this chapter divides them into six groups.

Paperwork

Problems with paperwork

Examples of this are:

- Missing invoice.

- No order number.

- Delivery address not specified.

- Lack of sufficient detail on invoice.

Recommended approach

Establish that there are no problems with the rest of the account and that other invoices (if any) will be paid on time.

Identify the problem with the invoice and get the customer to agree that, apart from the identified problem, the invoice is in order. If the problem is a missing order then, obviously, a copy should be sent at once. Do consider doing this by fax or e-mail.

Tell the customer that you will provide the missing information immediately (or specify the date when it will be provided). Then press the customer to say when it will be paid. You can tell the customer that payment is late (if it is), you will provide the missing information, and that you feel justified in asking for a special payment in the near future.

If the invoice is particularly big, particularly important, or is holding up a big payment, it is worth ringing to check that the missing information has actually arrived and that payment will be made.

If payment still does not come you should ring again, take a strong line and perhaps move on to your sanctions.

Comment

This may be annoying because customers' requirements can be very unreasonable. Nevertheless, you will usually have to do the work and provide the information.

If you are forever providing missing information you may need to examine your own systems. Perhaps improvements are necessary.

You may find some customers calling for extra information an unacceptable number of times. You will probably not want to call your customer a liar, even if he is, but you could say something that hints that you know what he is doing. Perhaps you could say something like 'Oh dear, we have sent so many copy invoices. It must be a fault at your end. Would you please send me £10,000 on account, and then the other couple of hundred when you have sorted it out? I know its right, but if it isn't I'll let you have it back.'

There is a very effective counter to a person who repeatedly asks for copy invoices when an account becomes due. Ring and say something like 'I want to head off the problem this month. It is due in ten day's time, so if you need a copy please say now. Then you'll have it to pay on the due date.'

If the customer makes excuses frequently it may be worth an approach to someone at a higher level. You could say that repeated problems are making it difficult to do business, and ask that in everyone's interest, attention be given to the problem.

Payment systems

Delay in customer's payment system

Examples of this are:

- Invoice received, but not approved.

- No one to sign cheques.

- Records with accountant.

- Computer failure.

Recommended approach

If possible, get the customer to agree the amount that is due for payment and is not being paid because of the problem.

If the problem is unapproved invoices, press for the remainder of the account to be paid at once.

Give what help you can according to the problem. For example, if an invoice has not been paid because of lost information, then provide duplicate information.

Get the customer to agree that the account will be paid the minute that the problem can be overcome.

If the problem is no one to sign the cheques you can safely disbelieve the customer. You are hearing a lie. Provision is always made for emergencies as I am sure happens in your own organisation. Try a jocular question and ask what would happen if the electricity company arrived to cut off the electricity supply. Listen to the answer then say that as there is not a problem with the electricity could you have that cheque please. Another good question is to ask if the staff are going to be paid that week.

If the account cannot be reconciled, ask for a large payment on account, with the remainder to follow shortly.

For some problems you can assure the customer that your religious beliefs do not compel you to take a computer-generated cheque. On this occasion you are willing to take a manual one.

'Books at the accountant' is almost by definition an excuse from a small customer, but do not accept it. Say that you know the accountant, will shortly be driving that way, and offer to bring them back. Offer to accept a manual cheque and offer to accept a large payment on account, with the balance to follow.

Be very persistent and keep asking. Nag them.

Comment

By definition, this must be the customer's fault. You are entitled to be cross, though perhaps you do not want to show it, and you are entitled to take a firm line. Be very persistent and if necessary embarrass them, remember:

- All customers have manual cheques.

- There is always provision for emergencies.

- There is always someone to sign (or pre-signed blank cheques).

- A payment on account is nearly as good.

Humour often gets you a long way. I was once in a restaurant that told a caller that they were fully booked and did not have a table available. The caller would not accept this and asked what would happen if the Prince of Wales arrived without a booking. The proprietor reluctantly conceded that they would squeeze him in. The caller then said that he had been watching the television news and the Prince was touring Australia, so it would be quite safe to let him have that table. After he had stopped laughing the proprietor agreed to find a place.

The story has no connection with credit control but it illustrates a point. It is the equivalent of asking what would happen if the electricity was being cut off.

Customer disputes payment terms that have been agreed

Recommended approach

- Agree the amount and age of the debt.

- Point out that the customer has accepted your terms. If necessary provide proof by sending a copy of the signed contract or other documentation. You should be able to do this, and your position will be much weaker if you cannot.

- Tell the customer politely, but firmly, that a certain payment period was part of the contract and that you must insist that the agreement is honoured.

- Ask the customer bluntly why he is reneging on an agreement. This is a very difficult question to answer without embarrassment. The only truthful answer is, presumably, that they have decided to take an unfair advantage.

If the customer still will not pay, you have to take a policy decision. You can:

a) Take steps to enforce the agreement. This could be suspension of supplies and the threat of legal action.

b) Give in and accept the customer's terms.

c) Try and negotiate a compromise.

If you do decide to give in and accept the customer's terms make it clear that you are holding them to the letter of those terms. If the customer says that he pays on 90 days ring at 9.01 am on the ninetieth day.

Comment

You are legally and morally in the right, so you are entitled to be annoyed. The customer is trying to cheat you. You should take a tough line and try to persuade the customer to honour the commitment. If he will not do so a policy decision on your part is unavoidable.

Customer will not accept terms that have not been agreed

Recommended approach

Agree the amount and age of the debt.

- Try and persuade the customer that your terms are fair, reasonable, normal in the industry, accepted by everyone else, and so on. You cannot quote the law or an agreement, so it will be a challenge to your negotiating skills. Your position will be much stronger if you are a key supplier, or if the customer is dependant on you.

- Without conceding anything get a firm promise for a certain date. Do not let them go beyond what they say their terms are.

Ultimately you may have to take a policy decision:

a) Take sanctions, perhaps close the account, perhaps say that future business can only be done on agreed terms, or

b) Give in and accept the customer's terms, or

c) Try and negotiate a compromise.

Comment

Your position is weak and you should not be in it. Terms should be agreed in advance. You will just have to do the best that you can. You must be silver-tongued and earn your salary.

Customer says that he cannot pay now

Note the word 'cannot'. He is not saying 'will not' he is saying 'cannot'. Sometimes this will be baldly put, but more usually euphemisms will be used. You will hear phrases like 'cash flow imbalance'. Sometimes the customer will be forth-coming, will co-operate and will say when he expects to make payment. Sometimes the customer will not give any information at all.

Recommended approach

- Always take the problem seriously.

- Agree amount and age of the debt.

- Insist on talking to a senior person.

- Try and get all the facts about what has gone wrong and why. Try and establish if it is a one-off problem or if it is likely to recur.

- Try and get a promised date for payment. Or at least try and get an indication of how the problem will be resolved.

- If the proposal is reasonable, and if you believe that the customer is making a good effort to solve the problem, you might agree to it. If so, monitor the account closely. If the promise is not kept you should contact the customer immediately and reconsider your position.

- If the customer will not give details or a clear commitment you will probably take a strong line and implement your sanctions, perhaps starting with a warning letter.The same applies if the customer makes an unacceptable proposal.

Comment

This situation is always worrying and should always be taken seriously. Judgment is called for. Personal knowledge of the customer, his character, and his track record is a big help, if available.

Some customers do go through a bad patch and deserve support. On the other hand, some customers have bad patch after bad patch after bad patch. Any credit controller is used to seeing the same names on the problem list year after year.

This section is devoted to customers who say that they cannot pay now. But of course most of them could if they really had to. It is very often a competitive situation and not everyone can necessarily be paid at once. Suppliers who take a tough line get paid quickly, and the more tolerant ones do not.

At this point it is worth summarising the law on wrongful trading by company directors. It is:

> *'Directors may be disqualified and be personally liable for debts if they carry on trading when they know, or ought to know, that there is no reasonable prospect of avoiding insolvent liquidation'.*

There are times when it pays to remind company directors of this.

Miscellaneous

Cheque is in the post

This is the oldest excuse in the book and you have probably heard it hundreds of times. Royal Mail is much maligned but generally gives a very reliable service. It may very occasionally be true but usually is not. At best 'in the post' usually means in the envelope ready to be posted. At worst it is a downright lie.

The response is to ask when the cheque was posted. After three days tell the customer that it has been lost in the post and ask for a duplicate to be sent immediately by first class mail. Watch very carefully for the 'duplicate' and get very cross if this one does not arrive quickly.

Already paid

You are advised to react carefully to the words 'already paid'. It may be true. How confident of your systems are you? And how confident are you of the work of your colleagues? Cheques do occasionally go unbanked. There are sometimes delays in posting the sales ledger. Most common of all, payments do get misallocated or posted to the wrong account.

The correct response is to ask the customer for precise details of how and when payment was made. If the customer cannot tell you, then you are entitled to be very suspicious indeed. If the customer does tell you, then you must check the facts thoroughly and establish whether it is true or not. This can be difficult as you may be looking for something that is not there. It is often easier if you work in cooperation with the customer. It sometimes happens that there is a genuine misunderstanding. The customer thinks that he has paid and you think that he has not.

Sometimes the customer will say that a cheque has been sent and will quote date, amount and cheque number. You, on the other hand, have no record of receiving it. You should then ask the customer to check his bank statement and advise you of the date that it was debited. You can normally take off two working days to find the date that it was banked. Even this is not absolutely conclusive. It may be a genuine cheque that has (accidentally or deliberately) been banked by someone else.

Technical fault with the cheque

Examples are:

- Not signed.

- Post dated.

- Words and figures differ.

The error may be accidental, but frequently it is not. You may spot the error before banking, or you may only find out several days later when the cheque is returned through the banking system.

The normal response is to send the cheque back to the customer for alteration with confirming signature. If the cheque has been rejected by the bank this may be the only option. If you do this you should not allow the customer long to send back the corrected cheque. Be very insistent that it is actioned quickly.

There is another way. That is to bank the cheque despite knowing that there is a fault. The changes in banking practices (many would say decline) are your ally on this occasion. Banks no longer scrutinise cheques in the way that they once did and there is a reasonable chance that the cheque will be paid despite the fault. The smaller the amount on the cheque the greater your chances. You will not be doing anything wrong. It is your money and the customer is hardly in a position to complain.

A variation on this is to photocopy the cheque, bank it, then ring the customer. You can tell the customer that you have noticed the 'inadvertant error', and ask him to give instructions to his bank to pay it on presentation. As banks do respond to such instructions, and as the customer claims that it was an innocent mistake, he will find it difficult to refuse this request. It is best to ring after the cheque has actually been banked. This may be the best solution for large cheques that are more likely to be scrutinised by the paying bank.

There is a final possibility when the words and figures on the cheque differ. This is to get your bank to mark the cheque '*Lower Amount Claimed*'. Bank practices differ but many banks will do this, and many paying banks will accept a cheque marked in this way. Having obtained payment of the lower amount you can write off the difference (if the higher amount was the correct figure and the difference is small) or you can ask the customer to pay it. The customer has made the 'mistake' and is not in a good position to complain.

Checklist

✓ Do be very sceptical. However, do remember that the customer just might be telling the truth. This is particularly the case when the customer says that payment has already been made.

✓ Do try to isolate the problem then press the customer to pay everything else.

✓ Do consider pressing for a large payment on account. This is often a very reasonable request.

✓ Do be prepared to spend time helping the customer with further information. It may be unfair but it is usually in your interest to do it.

✓ Do be very persistent (nag if necessary). Do not let things drag on.

✓ Do take a hard line if the fault is with the customer's systems. By definition, the problem cannot be your fault. This is a good case to press for a large payment on account.

✓ Do consider using humour and do consider using embarrassment. Witty examples are in this chapter.

✓ Do remember that all customers have manual cheques, and all customers make provision for emergencies. Anyone who says differently is not telling the truth.

✓ Do always take it seriously when a customer says that payment 'cannot' be made now. Do insist on speaking to a senior person.

✓ Do remember that you should have agreed terms in advance. If you have done so you are legally and morally in the right. Nevertheless, a policy decision may be unavoidable.

✓ Do realise that your position is weak if you have not agreed terms in advance. You have a problem – do the best you can.

✓ Do consider using your knowledge of the banking system. Details are at the end of this chapter.

chapter nine

Sources of information

Introduction

Good information is a vital commodity. It is particularly important when a new account is first opened, but is of continuing importance thereafter. Following are some of the ways in which good information may be obtained:

Obtaining good information

Credit agencies

This is probably the main source of good information. It is so important that it deserves, and gets, a chapter all to itself. This is Chapter 10.

Trade references

This is covered in detail in Chapter 4. It is possible to manipulate trade references, but despite this they yield useful information in a high proportion of cases. It is surprisingly common to seek a trade reference, then ignore an unsatisfactory reply or the lack of a reply at all. This is a bad mistake. It may well be worth following up with a telephone call.

Bank references

This is covered in detail in Chapter 4. A bank reference may give helpful information about the soundness of a customer. It is unlikely to indicate how promptly the customer pays its bills.

Companies House

One of the prices of limited liability is that companies have to place certain information on public record. This information includes:

- Annual accounts (audited for all but the smallest companies).

- Identity of all directors (information includes full name, address and details of other directorships held within the previous five years).

- Registered charges on assets.

- The Annual Return (this includes the name and address of all shareholders, although these may be nominees).

Annual accounts of a PLC must be filed within seven months of the accounting reference date. Annual accounts of a private company must be filed within ten months of the accounting reference date. Information relating to directors must be updated within 14 days of a relevant change.

This information, and more too, must be supplied to the Registrar of Companies at Companies House. The Registrar places it all on public record. Appendix B to this Guide gives further information about Companies House. In particular, it gives the addresses and telephone numbers of its various offices, further details of information available, and details of charges made.

Information may be obtained from Companies House by personal application, but it is more usual to use the services of an agent. Many agents provide an excellent and moderately priced service. An essential step to identifying the correct company is to obtain the company registration number. It is a legal requirement that this be printed on all company note paper. There is an alphabetical index at Companies House but there are more than a million names on it. So, the correct number will probably save time and trouble.

There used to be a serious problem with companies not filing information and filing late. It still happens, but the situation is much improved. Computerisation, automatic penalties, and better enforcement have all played a part. However, by definition, information is filed after the event. Accounts are always out-of-date, even if promptly filed and recently checked.

Only companies have to file information at Companies House. The obligation does not extend to sole traders and partnerships.

Trade sources and your competitors

In many cases this is the most valuable source of all. Your contacts will be in the same business, and often will be known to you personally. You will develop experience of their reliability and the way in which they express their opinions. They are likely to be receiving similar favours from you and are likely to be forthcoming for this reason.

Many businesses belong to a trade association, Chamber of Commerce, or similar grouping which may be the basis of an exchange of information. In some cases, staff will have friends and former colleagues working for competitors. It can be very valuable to make contact with your opposite number in other firms. Even though you are competitors you will have a common interest in avoiding bad debts and slow payers.

In many trades your customer is highly likely to have dealings with some of your competitors, and the chances of obtaining useful information are therefore high. Such pooling of knowledge can be particularly valuable when the payment performance of an established customer is deteriorating. You will usually find that your competitors are experiencing the same problems. Sometimes a combined approach to the customer can be in the best interests of everyone (including the customer).

The best results will be obtained if you keep in mind the following:

- Do not abuse the network by asking too often.

- Do not tell the customer about the exchange of information.

- Be reasonably forthcoming when asked yourself.

- Do not use the information to take an advantage over the person who supplied it.

Credit insurance

It may be possible to insure some or all of your debts against the risk of insolvency. This is covered in detail in Chapter 12.

The insurance companies make profits by having good information, by assessing risks and by making good judgments. They are very good at it and they do not get it wrong very often. If you are refused insurance for a customer, or a high rate is quoted, then you should think hard about the possible implications.

If you have a good relationship with an insurance company you will probably be able to discuss individual problems. The insurance company may even give informal advice on a debt that is not being insured. This advice can be extremely valuable and contacts are well worth cultivating.

In-house opinion

You will best get the benefit of this mine of information if you cultivate an atmosphere where staff talk freely and exchange opinions. Do not complain if a warning in good faith turns out to be unjustified. The next warning may be vital and well-founded. In particular, it is important that sales departments and accounts departments have a good working relationship. It is often the sales department that is best placed to hear disturbing rumours or see what is happening at customers' premises.

You should take notice of telling phrases such as:

- 'Not much stock about.'

- 'A lot of staff leaving.'

- 'They're desperate for us to take the order.'

There may be a good explanation for these comments but they should put you on your guard.

Your own records

It is human nature not to fully value what is freely available and under one's own nose. Once an account has been established for some time your own sales ledger, and other records, will be a mine of useful information. In fact they will be so valuable that others will seek references from you.

Your own sales ledger will tell you whether the customer normally pays to terms, and if not how bad the record is. It will tell you whether settlement discounts are normally taken if they are available. Failure to take a worthwhile settlement discount is either a sign of ineptitude or a shortage of working capital.

Perhaps most significant of all, it will tell you whether the customer's payment performance is deteriorating, stable or improving. A deteriorating payment performance is often a very bad sign, sometimes worse than a consistently bad record.

Checklist

✓ Do constantly tell yourself that good information is vital.

✓ Do remember that credit agencies can often give you very good information.

✓ Do realise that despite their drawbacks, trade references are very useful. On no account should you ignore a bad reply or a failure to reply.

✓ Do realise that bank references may help avoid a bad debt, but may not be much help in spotting a slow payer.

✓ Do not forget that annual accounts for all companies may be obtained from Companies House. Details of directors, and shareholders, and other information is also available.

✓ Do remember that using a credit agent may be the most efficient and economical way of getting information from Companies House.

✓ Do consider trade sources and especially do consider exchanging information with competitors. This is often very fruitful and you will be able to help each other.

✓ Do respect credit insurers; they usually get it right. It pays to cultivate a good relationship with your insurer.

✓ Do encourage open relationships within your own organisation. Encourage people to express their opinions about credit and customers. Listen to these opinions. It is especially important that the sales department talks to the accounts department, and vice versa.

✓ Do not undervalue the information in your own records. Especially note if the customer's payment record is deteriorating, and if the customer fails to take a worthwhile settlement discount (if available).

chapter ten

Credit agencies

Introduction

Although this chapter is entitled credit agencies, its scope is a little wider and encompasses advice, information and services provided by credit and information specialists. The latter part of this chapter lists and studies the services that are available. But we will start with an overall review of the agencies and their services, together with advice on how to get the best value.

Choosing the right agency

There are over 150 credit agencies in the UK and, as you would expect, their standards and costs vary quite a bit. It is therefore worth some care to select the one or two most likely to give the best results.

Some agencies specialise in particular trades or regions. Local or trade enquiries will probably produce good recommendations. Similarly, some agencies only offer certain services or specialise in certain areas.

If you have a large business selling to different trades across the county, you will probably do best with one of the large agencies with familiar names. Dun and Bradstreet and Intrum Justita are well-known examples. Some of the large agencies offer an international dimension as well as UK services. They might not give the best result in every individual case but are likely to give good average results. This is not to belittle the smaller agencies. They may not offer every service, but you probably do not want every service.

I recommend occasionally putting the same enquiry to more than one agency. You will be able to compare the results and form an opinion as to which one is the more reliable and useful. This can hardly be done with collections and legal action as it would confuse the customer. One can, though, put different cases to different agencies and see which does the best.

Credit agency charges

Some agencies ask for subscriptions on a regular basis and with a guarantee of a certain number of enquiries. This is often financed by prepaying for a certain number of cases, usually in the form of a book of vouchers. Other agencies are happy to supply information on a one-off basis and to charge accordingly.

There has in the past been some controversy over the charging methods of one or two agencies. Customers complained that they were misled into prepaying for more services than they needed. This no longer seems to be such a problem, but it is worth checking the point. You certainly should not pay for more services that you will actually use. It is a competitive market and charges are, on the whole, reasonable.

Failings of credit agencies

Do not make the mistake of thinking that credit agencies are infallible, and if it is written down it must be right. A personal experience illustrates the point powerfully.

Some years ago I accepted an introductory offer of three free status enquiries from an agency soliciting my business. I gave them the names of two new customers and an existing customer whom I thought I knew well. This customer had a long trading record with me. He sometimes paid a little slowly but I had never had any serious worries. At the time of making the enquiry he owed £80,000. The reply included the following:

'*...cause for concern. We recommend that no more than £500 credit be granted and that the position be reviewed in three month's time.*'

I took a deep breath then decided to ignore the report, taking the view that I knew more about my customer than the agency did. Happily, my confidence was not misplaced (if it had been I would not be telling the story). Several years of mutually profitable trading followed, and there were no problems.

As with trade references, you may know best about your existing customers. My experience related above is terrible for the reputation of credit agencies, but it was only one agency on one occasion. Sometimes agencies are proved spectacularly right when events justify their caution. This can happen some time after the warning.

Reasons for problems

A problem for agencies is that few people remember the hundreds of times when they give a favourable report and the advice is sound. On the other hand their embarrassment is very public when a business fails shortly after having received a good recommendation. A possible tendency towards caution may be understandable.

If you have serious doubts about an opinion it may be worth asking the same question of another agency. Factual information should, of course, be correct and there is normally no point in double checking it.

A problem may occur because the agent has not done a good job, but insufficient or out-of-date information is more likely to be a problem.

Insufficient information is particularly likely with businesses only having a short trading record. Accounts and other information may not yet be available at Companies House, and the shortness of the trading record may make it difficult to obtain useful references. In these circumstances the information may be limited and the agent will probably recommend caution. You just have to use your judgment and the information that you have.

Of course, established companies sometimes file accounts and other information late, though the problems are no longer as severe as they once were. Companies House has improved its enforcement performance. Experience shows that companies that file late may not be a good credit risk, and the credit agency will probably make this recommendation. Good news tends to get published quickly and bad news tends to get published slowly.

How up-to-date the published accounts are is of course influenced by the time of year that the question is posed. PLCs must file within seven months of the balance sheet date, and private companies must file within ten months of the balance sheet date. Take for example a private company that makes up its accounts each December 31st. An enquiry at Companies House on 30th October 1998 must (by law) disclose the accounts for the year to December 31st 1996. An enquiry at Companies House on November 1st 1998 must (by law) disclose the accounts for the year to December 31st 1997.

Methods of obtaining information

You may obtain information from your credit agent by post, but delay may be a problem if time is important. For an extra fee a prompt response may be given by telex or fax. Most agencies now have facilities for on-line access to their data base. This is marvellous but do not be dazzled by the technology. The information will be just as good, or just as bad, as if it had been obtained by traditional methods.

When to use credit agencies

It is a competitive business and services are usually reasonably priced. Nevertheless, cost considerations must to some extent limit the use of credit agencies. An obvious time to get an opinion is when a new account is opened. Other times are when a particularly big order is obtained, and especially when you have become worried for some reason. Warning signs are covered in Chapter 14 but some possibilities are:

- A change for the worse in the payments pattern. This is usually the most worrying sign, and the most often encountered.

- An intuitive feeling that is based on contact with the customer.

- Sight of worrying published accounts, knowledge that accounts are late, or knowledge that the customer is using creative accountancy.

- Worrying press comment.

- Customer making repeated mistakes with cheques.

- People being difficult to contact and failing to ring back. This is especially worrying if it is a person who is normally helpful.

- Receipt of round sum payments on account.

- Empty shelves and/or unnaturally large orders.

- High staff turnover.

- A worrying exchange of information with a competitor, or from another trade source.

How to best use a credit agency

Never forget that you are interested in the speed at which an account is likely to be paid, as well as its potential to be a bad debt. Many companies, particularly large companies, are very safe and very slow. At my credit control seminars the names of certain companies are raised time and again. The complaints relate to the abysmal slowness of payment rather than to the safety of the debt.

You may well receive an alarmingly large amount of detail from your credit agent. You should look on this as a 'good fault' and learn to disregard the superfluous.

You should take care to give accurate and precise information to the credit agency. There are over a million companies on the register at Companies House and many have very similar names. If you do not get it exactly right you may receive a report on the wrong one and, even worse, perhaps not realise it. Every company has a unique registration number which must, by law, be shown on company stationery. It is a good idea to quote this number to the credit agent.

You may get best results from the credit agent if you ask specific questions. Mention precise sums for the amount of credit proposed.

Details of services available

The following is a long list of the main services provided by credit agents. Of course not all services are available from every agent, but many of the bigger ones provide most of them. When studying the list, please remember that some agents specialise in consumer debt, some in trade debt, and some are equally good in both areas.

Collection services

Agents will take over the collection of some or all debts and endeavour to obtain payment. They will do this by means of letters, telephone calls and perhaps other methods as well. It is often claimed that contact from a third party puts psychological pressure on the customer. The debtor is apt to think that you are serious about obtaining payment, and may fear that slow payment would damage his credit standing. Both fears are probably justified.

The credit agent may charge a fee or receive a percentage of the sum recovered. A disadvantage is that it is another link in the chain if there are disputes or queries about the account. The credit agent will have to refer them to you which is time consuming and slows down collection. Third party collecting is most suited to clean, uncomplicated debts. It is usual to agree in advance what methods will be used and at what intervals.

Legal action to recover debts

This goes one stage further. Sometimes it is an authorised extension of other collection procedures. Sometimes debts are only passed to the agent when other methods have failed and legal action is required. As with other collection services, payment is sometimes by a fee and sometimes by a percentage of the sum recovered.

The credit agent will deal with a large volume of cases, and will probably process the paperwork efficiently, using computerised systems. Some credit agents employ solicitors. The credit agent will probably advise on the best methods to obtain judgment and to enforce judgment if payment is still not forthcoming. It may advise on the chances of success.

Door to door collection

Some agents employ old-fashioned door to door collectors. This is an extension of the collection services described above.

International collection

A few agents will take action in foreign courts, and will endeavour to enforce judgment obtained in a British court. This can be difficult (or virtually impossible – depending on the country) and very specialised credit agents that are part of an international group have certain advantages. Remember, that for this purpose, Scotland is a foreign country.

Debt purchase

Some agents will purchase debts from you. This has the advantage that it is a clear cut solution and you get immediate payment. The amount that you get will be a negotiated percentage of the total debt. The agent will then take action to enforce the debt and will get all the benefits if it succeeds.

Continued monitoring

Sometimes collection methods fail, perhaps because the customer just has not got the money to pay. Some credit agencies will continue to monitor the customer and reactivate the collection, perhaps years later, if his financial position improves.

Recovery and repossession

The agent will endeavour to recover such things as leased goods, goods on hire purchase, credit cards and cheque books.

Tracing services

The agent will endeavour to find people or businesses that have gone missing.

Debt counselling

It is the debtor (individual or business) that is counselled, not you. However, it is partly (or mainly) for your benefit. The object is to help the troubled debtor draw up a realistic and sustainable repayment plan.

Personal reports

This is a report on individuals, sole traders and partnerships. The report may give details of such things as county court Judgments and bankruptcy proceedings. It may be combined with a credit rating.

Company report

This may well be the most used service. It may include such things as:

- Incorporation details.

- Names of Directors and Company Secretary.

- Turnover and profit.

- Asset, liabilities and ratios.

- An assessment of how long the company takes to pay a typical debt.

The report may include a recommendation on the amount of credit that should be granted.

Report on Directors

This is a full report on the Directors of a company and would include such things as:

- Full name.

- Private address.

- Date of birth.

- Date of appointment.

- Other directorships currently held and ones that have been held during the previous five years.

Consultancy and training

You may receive advice on your credit control systems, and receive training for credit control staff.

Professional representation at creditors' meeting

The agent may attend on your behalf and provide an independent report afterwards. He will cast your vote by proxy either using his own judgment or in accordance with your instructions. Some agencies may do this without charge. It may pay to ask.

Bailiff services

This is self-explanatory.

Process servicing

This assists in the prompt and effective servicing of writs and other legal documents. As we will see in the chapters on legal action, this can be a problem. Debtors sometimes claim that documents have not been properly served.

Credit rating

The credit agent will give a points 'score' depending on a weighting of all known factors. Interpretation of the score will give an indication of whether the customer is a good or bad credit risk. Dun and Bradstreet is a well known example of an agent that does this.

Checklist

✓ Do make local and trade enquiries when choosing the most suitable agency.

✓ Do consider using one of the big agencies if you have a wide spread of customers and need a variety of services.

✓ Do consider occasionally putting an enquiry to more than one agent. It may be useful to compare the results.

✓ Do realise that (fortunately) it is a very competitive business. Watch prices and do not make prepayments for unwanted services.

✓ Do realise that credit agencies are not infallible and that occasionally you may know better.

✓ However, do be very careful. They may be right after all, and you may discover it later to your cost.

✓ Do remember that information may be unsatisfactory, or incomplete, in the case of a recently formed company or a business that has not been trading for long.

✓ Do consider using fax or on-line access.

✓ Do consider using credit agencies for new accounts, when there is an expansion in business, when payment performance deteriorates and when something worries you about an account.

✓ Do remember that you are not just interested in the bad debt risk. Promptness of payment is also important.

✓ Do identify your customer carefully. There are over a million companies on the register.

✓ Do ask specific questions and mention amounts.

✓ Do understand that customers may react positively to third party involvement in the collection process. They may take you more seriously and they may want to protect their credit standing.

✓ Do remember that a wide range of services are available, mostly competitively priced. Study this chapter; you may not be aware of them all.

chapter eleven

Factoring

Introduction

Some years ago factoring had something of an image problem. Many people saw it as a lender of last resort and therefore tended to be rather wary of businesses that used it. There never was very much justification for this view, and there is now no justification at all.

Factoring is an accepted, respectable source of finance. Other services (including sales ledger, credit control and bad debt insurance) may be available. In appropriate cases I recommend that you give it serious consideration.

Factoring is a way of getting up-front finance on invoiced sales and this is its main attraction for most of its customers. Depending on the type of service negotiated, the factoring company may also maintain the sales ledger, operate credit control procedures, take the bad debt risk and offer informal advice and support.

For convenience, factoring services may be divided into three broad categories as follows:

Non-recourse and recourse factoring

Non-recourse factoring

The factoring company will advance up to about 85% of invoices issued to approved customers. This can normally be done within 24 hours of the issue of the invoice.

The factoring company takes the bad debt risk. Please note that it is insuring against bad debts, not against slow payment. It will accept the risk of specified events such as liquidation, total disappearance, etc. It will of course take over your rights against the customer, and keep any amounts that can ultimately be recovered.

The existence of factoring is usually disclosed to the customer who is asked to pay directly to the factoring company. When this is done the factoring company will deduct its fees, then forward the percentage of the invoice not originally advanced. The factoring company will maintain the sales ledger, send out statements and operate credit control procedures.

It is normal for the existence of factoring to be disclosed to the customer. However, some factoring companies offer a service where this does not happen. If factoring is not disclosed, the factoring company does not send out statements and does not operate credit control procedures. If factoring is not disclosed the customer will pay the business issuing the invoice. The appropriate sum must then be forwarded to the factoring company.

Recourse factoring

This operates in the same way as non-recourse factoring, but the factoring company does not take the bad debt risk. For this reason it is likely to be slightly cheaper. A specified time is agreed and if payment has not been received by the due date, then the client must reimburse the factor with the amount advanced.

Invoice discounting

Invoice discounting is technically not factoring at all, but it is very similar. It is purely a secured financial advance with no administrative help or maintenance of the sales ledger. It is the fastest growing sector in factoring.

The working of invoice discounting is best illustrated with an example. Let us suppose that your sales ledger totals £1,000,000. The factoring company will take a legal charge over all the debts, then write a cheque for say 80% (£800,000). You will pay interest and a fee, but so long as the total sales ledger stays at £1,000,000 no further advance will be made.

If at the end of a month the total sales ledger balance has grown to £1,200,000, the factoring company will advance a further £160,000 (80% x £200,000). If at the end of the following month the total sales ledger balance has dropped to £900,000 you must pay £240,000 to the factoring company (80% x £300,000). This series of monthly adjustments will continue until the arrangement is terminated, when the whole outstanding balance must be repaid. Of course the fee and interest are payable.

Some of the features of factoring

All the factoring companies run efficient modern systems. They have to do this to maintain efficiency, provide service to their clients and keep on top of the vast number of transactions that they handle. Many of the companies provide a facility for on-line access. You are thus able to easily check your sales ledger and all the records.

Factoring is only available for business to business debts. It is not available for consumer debts.

Some factoring companies provide the service for sales to overseas customers. This may be particularly valuable as assistance with debt collection may be especially useful. The factoring companies may employ specialists with linguistic skills.

The factoring companies are very well financed. They nearly all have links to financial institutions and some are subsidiaries of the major clearing banks.

The costs tend (in my opinion) to be reasonable. These are set out towards the end of this chapter.

The percentage of finance that may be available

This will be negotiated on a case by case basis. Relevant factors will include:

- Your own reputation and financial standing.

- An assessment of the risks posed by your customers. The factor will want to know if the risks are concentrated or widely distributed.

- The overall size of the finance sought.

Depending on circumstances, up to about 85% of each invoice may be available. In the case of invoice discounting up to about 80% of the total sales ledger (after realistic bad debt and other reserves) may be available.

The minimum level of turnover required

Alex Lawrie looks for the following (figures include VAT):

- Factoring – at least £50,000 p.a.

- Disclosed Invoice Discounting – at least £300,000 per year.

- Confidential Invoice Discounting – at least £500,000 per year.

Difficult or unlikely business

Alex Lawrie (to whom I am grateful for this and certain other information) specifies:

- Those in the building industry and firms which have to invoice for work-in-progress during the contract.

- Those producing garments for the 'cheaper end' of the clothing market.

- Those who derive turnover from advertising in free issue newspapers.

- Those who sell principally to members of the public.

- Those whose business is subject to disputes and a high level of credit notes.

This is a fascinating list and is thought-provoking for everyone involved in credit management. It is not a recommendation for the building and garment industries.

Advantages and disadvantages of factoring

Advantages

Most factoring clients use the services because it is a boost to cash flow from next to immediate payment of invoices. Other reasons are all very well, but this one predominates. Customers want the money. And why not? For many businesses unpaid invoices represent the biggest asset item in their balance sheet.

- It is a competitive business and the services are competitively priced.

- Many businesses find the credit control support particularly helpful for export business.

- In appropriate cases (and where negotiated) bad debt cover is extremely helpful.

- Many customers respect third party involvement, and factoring is one form of third party involvement. They may believe that the factoring company is efficient and unlikely to be swayed by excuses. They may also fear that their credit reputation will suffer if they delay payment.

- Factoring companies have advanced and efficient systems.

- Many people have found that the introduction of a factoring company has forced them to get their own systems and sales ledger in order. They could have done it anyway, and should have done it anyway, but the factoring company was the catalyst that forced them to do it.

- Factoring companies are usually willing to offer informal advice and encouragement. They will be a source of good information about potentially troublesome customers.

Disadvantages

Costs are reasonable, but nothing is for nothing. It has to be paid for.

- It is an extra link in the chain. Even when things work smoothly this is a drawback. Disputes and queries have to be referred back. This costs time and money. Factoring is most suited to clean, uncomplicated debts. Factoring companies have advanced and efficient systems, but they are operated by human beings who can make mistakes. The extra link in the chain can increase the problems caused by human mistakes.

- The ultimate customer will be instructed (if factoring is disclosed) to pay directly to the factoring company. Despite this, some will continue to pay you. This causes extra work.

- The boost to cash flow is real, but the overall effect may well be less than at first supposed. This is because the factor will take a legal charge on the debts, and the value of security that can be offered to another borrower is therefore reduced. A clearing bank, for example, may seek a reduction in overdraft facilities. However, the reduction in the overdraft facility is not likely to be as great as the extra cash released by the factoring.

Costs

This will vary according to circumstances, the size of the transaction, the degree of perceived risk etc. The following is a reasonable guide:

- Factoring of invoices – fee of between 0.5% and 3.0% of turnover. In addition interest of between 2.0% and 3.0% over base rate whilst the money is advanced.

- Disclosed Invoice Discounting – fee of between 0.1% and 1.0% of turnover. In addition interest between 2.0% and 3.0% over base rate on the balance outstanding.

- Undisclosed Invoice Discounting – fee of between 0.1% and 0.75% of turnover. In addition interest between 1.5% and 2.5% over base rate on the balance outstanding.

It may well be worth negotiating on charges and getting quotes from more than one company. A small percentage of a large sum is worth saving.

Detailed example of a factoring transaction

ABC Ltd had negotiated a fee of 2.0% of turnover and interest over base rate of 2.5% (assume base rate of 7.0% making 9.5% in all). Factor advances 80% of invoice value.

Invoice for £10,000 issued on February 1st. Factor pays ABC Ltd on February 2nd. Customer pays Factor on March 2nd.

What happens is as follows:

February 1st:	Invoice for £10,000 issued.
February 2nd:	Factor sends £8,000 to ABC Ltd.
March 2nd:	Customer pays £10,000 to Factor.
March 3rd:	Factor sends £1,736.67 to ABC Ltd.

This figures of £1,736.67 is calculated as follows:

Balance of invoice	£2,000.00
Less fee (2.0% of £10,000)	£200.00
	£1,800.00
Less interest	
(1 month x £8,000 x 9.5%)	£63.33
	£1,736.67

Checklist

✓ Do seriously consider factoring in appro-priate cases. It very often gives good service and good value.

✓ Do remember that factoring is an excellent way of releasing money tied up in trade debtors, often the biggest figure on the assets side of the balance sheet.

✓ Do value the cover against bad debt risk.

✓ Do consider if invoice discounting is what you really want.

✓ Do especially consider factoring for export debts.

✓ Do negotiate on fees. It is a competitive business and it may pay to shop around.

✓ Do value the third party involvement in chasing payment. It helps with some customers.

✓ Do value the informal advice that a factor may offer.

see over

✓ Do remember that factoring is most suited to clean uncomplicated debts. Disputes and queries can cause delay and problems.

✓ Do remember that a factoring company will take legal security over the debts. This will reduce the security that can be offered to other lenders, and may reduce borrowing from other sources.

chapter twelve

Credit insurance

Introduction

I have always followed the principle that it is wise to insure against catastrophe but not against misfortune, and I recommend this to anyone considering credit insurance. Such a person should first consider the size and spread of his debts. Secondly he should consider the effect on his business should the worst happen. This chapter commences with a summarised view of when you should, and should not, consider credit insurance.

Considering credit insurance

Circumstances when you probably should *not* consider credit insurance

If there are not large debts but just a great number of individual small debts, it is probably a mistake to take out credit insurance. This is because, barring a series of events amounting to a statistical freak of unbelievable proportions, no combination of failures would have a catastrophic effect on the business. Over a period of time the premiums paid would probably add up to an amount similar to the money returned in the form of claims. As insurance companies have expenses, and usually make a profit, the premiums would probably be slightly larger than the claims.

This advice should, of course, be reconsidered, if the individually small debts are concentrated within one sector of the market or one geographic region. To take an example, suppose you make supplies to South African wine producers, and that all your debts are individually small amounts owing by South African companies. You will be vulnerable to a general downturn in the wine trade, and a problem (such as a crop disease) affecting specifically the South African wine trade. You will also be vulnerable to political and economic events affecting South Africa. In these circumstances you would be well advised to consider credit insurance.

Also, credit insurance may not be considered necessary if your own business is very soundly financed. This reasoning is even more compelling if your business is soundly financed and large, or you are part of a large group. This is because the failure of one or more of your larger customers would not seriously damage your company.

Insurance companies, very understandably, require their clients to follow certain credit procedures. If you deviate from them you may invalidate the cover. If you are unwilling to be bound by this, and prefer informal methods, then credit insurance may not be right for you. Needless to say this may be a dangerous line to adopt. Credit insurers require these policies for a reason, and it may be that you disregard them at your peril. Often, one of the benefits of involving third parties (this includes factors, etc) is that it forces you to put your records and systems in good order. This could just as well have been done anyway, but third party involvement forces you to do it.

Circumstances when you should consider credit insurance

The circumstances in which you should seriously consider credit insurance are those in which the above do not apply.

Overwhelmingly, you should seriously consider credit insurance if the failure of one customer, or a small number of customers, would have a catastrophic effect on your own business. 'Catastrophe' is an extreme word so let us also say that you should seriously consider credit insurance if such a failure, or failures, would have a significantly adverse effect on your business.

You should seriously consider credit insurance if your business is small and/or not soundly financed. In these circumstances the premiums will probably be more of a burden, but the need is definitely greater.

You may consider credit insurance as part of overall credit strategy. Credit insurance is commonly included in a factoring agreement, and credit insurers offer detailed advice on sound credit policies. They also offer detailed advice on the credit standing of individual customers. Credit insurers are staking their own money and their information tends to be very good. This is a valuable benefit.

Perhaps one should ask why debts should not be insured. After all, many other business assets are insured and trade debtors constitute an average of about 40% of current assets. Premises and fixed assets are usually insured. Stock is usually insured, even when it is dispersed, and even when it is in the course of delivery. Why not insure the debts as well? As it says elsewhere in this Guide '*There is no profit until the money is in the bank*'.

Selection of risks to be insured

It is normal to insure all accounts, or at least whole sections of them. An acquaintance of mine publishes textbooks which she sells to Local Education Authorities and also to book shops. She regards the Local Education Authorities as slow payers but totally safe, and she does not insure this sector of her accounts. However, she does not have the same confidence in the book shops and she does insure this sector.

Insurance companies do not generally permit 'cherry picking'. This is the selection of the debts most likely to be bad debts. This is a shame but you can, of course, understand their reasons. They are in the business to make a profit.

You can usually pick one large account for insurance, or a very small number of large accounts. If one customer accounts for 60% of turnover, then it would be reasonable to insure just that one account. The same would probably be true of two customers accounting for 30% each. Insurance companies will accept this as well as whole sectors.

Credit Insurance is a specialised and competitive business. It may pay to shop around and enquire exactly what the companies are willing to cover. Insurance brokers may be particularly useful in finding appropriate cover in this way. Of course, there may be a price to be paid. The worse the risk, or the combination of risks, the higher the premiums are likely to be.

Insuring only the large debts can in practice be achieved by agreeing a relatively high policy excess. Suppose that one customer normally owes £100,000 and ten other customers normally owe about £10,000 each. By agreeing to pay the first £15,000 of any claim you are in practice excluding all but the one largest account. The premiums will reflect this. A benefit will be that you are automatically insured if circumstances change. Perhaps one of the smaller accounts will grow or perhaps you will be the victim of a fraud.

Risks that can be covered

An extraordinarily wide range of risks may be covered. In most cases you will be primarily concerned with the insolvency of the buyer, or the buyer, even if not actually insolvent, being unable to pay you. In addition you may want to insure against the buyer being unwilling to pay you. However, policies, especially for export accounts, can go much further than this. For example, the following is a summary published by NCM Credit Insurance Ltd, to explain the categories of loss covered by its Compact policy:

Causes of loss covered	*You are covered if:*
Insolvency	any of your buyers becomes insolvent. Insolvency occurs if:

- a bankruptcy, winding-up, or administration order is made against the buyer

  or

- the execution of a judgment fails to satisfy the debt in full *or*

- a valid assignment, composition or other arrangement is made for the benefit of the buyer's creditors generally

or

- an effective resolution is passed to wind-up the buyer

or

- an administrative or other receiver or manager of any of the buyer's property is appointed

or

- you show, to our satisfaction, that the buyer's financial state is such that even partial payment is unlikely and that to enforce judgment or to apply for a bankruptcy or winding-up order would be disproportionate to the likely cost of the proceedings

or

- an event has occurred elsewhere than in England which, under the law of the court having jurisdiction, is substantially equivalent in effect to any of the events listed above.

Default   A buyer does not pay you the amount owing under the contract within six months of original due date of payment.

Moratorium   A moratorium on payment is decreed by the government of the buyer's country, or by that or a third country through which payment must be made.

Contract frustration	Any other measure or decision of a foreign government prevents, in whole or in part, performance of the contract.
Transfer	Political events, economic difficulties, legislative or administrative measures prevent or delay the transfer of payment or deposits made in respect of the contract.
Discharge of debt	A law operates in the buyer's country so as to give him a valid discharge of the debt under that law but not under the contract, even though the payments made, when converted to the currency of the contract, are less than the amount of debt at the date of transfer, because of exchange rate fluctuations.
War	War (including civil war, hostilities, rebellion and insurrection) revolution or riot, cyclone, flood, earthquake, volcanic eruption or tidal wave occurs outside your country and prevents in whole or in part performance of the contract.
Public buyer default	A public buyer fails or refuses to fulfil any of the terms of the contract. This cause of loss will only apply where we have stated in the credit limit that the buyer is a public buyer.

The same document goes on to list the following exclusions (all of which are defined in detail):

- Trade disputes.

- Failure by the insured to fulfil the terms of the contract.

- Failure to obtain a necessary licence.

- Third country involvement.

- Radioactivity.

- War involving specified countries.

This is just one such policy. Many other companies are in the business (and indeed other policies are available from NCM). Different types of cover may be available. It pays to shop around.

Credit insurance is normally only available for business to business sales, not for consumer debt.

Financial provisions in detail

In virtually all cases the insured is required to take part of the risk. It may be a small part (around 5%) or it may be more. Obviously, the higher the excess, the lower the premium. This is normal practice, and it gives the insured an incentive not to take silly risks and to adopt vigorous credit control procedures.

Premium terms will be quoted for example as 30p per cent for 75% cover. This means that if annual turnover is £100,000 then the annual premium will be £300.

In the event of a total loss on an account owing £10,000 the pay out would be £7,500. If the failed customer pays 50p in the pound then the insurance pay out will be £10,000 x 50% x 75% = £3,750. If any dividends from the debt are made after the insurance pay out they will go 25% to the insurance company and 75% to its client.

A guide to the cost of credit insurance

Credit insurance is a competitive business and it pays to shop around. Cost is influenced by a number of factors; among them the following:

- Your own standing.

- The standing of your customers.

- The spread of risks.

- The sector of the market. Some sectors (such as small builders) are rated badly.

- The size of business placed.

- The percentage of the risk retained by the insured.

- The precise definition of cover required.

As a guide, Trade Indemnity plc say that the premium is usually calculated as a percentage of the turnover, and that the percentage ranges from 0.1% to 1.0%. However, in most cases the premium is between 0.3% and 0.7%.

Working with credit insurance

Credit insurance should be regarded as complementary to good credit control. On no account should it be regarded as a substitute for it. Bad debts are bad for any business even if they are insured, and bad credit control may be punished in the following ways:

- A bad claims record may result in higher premiums.

- Credit insurance does not give total cover. Part of the debt, perhaps just a small part, must be borne by the client.

- Bad credit control results in slow payment with the resultant interest costs to the business.

It is very often possible to establish a very good relationship with one's credit insurance company. They succeed by being very good indeed at assessing risks and their opinions should be taken very seriously. Unlike credit agencies they back their judgment with their own money. They may well be willing to give informal advice to an established customer and this is well worth pursuing if it is available.

If an account is refused, the implications should be squarely faced. An insurance company makes money by accepting premiums. If it refuses premiums it does so for what it considers to be good reasons. If you accept business despite this warning, you should have good reasons and be aware of the risks.

Checklist

✓ Do consider my advice to insure against catastrophe, but not necessarily against misfortune.

✓ Do remember that it will probably not be wise to insure if you have a large spread of individually small debts. However, watch a possible concentration on one sector or area.

✓ Do remember that insurance may be less necessary if you are large (or part of a large group) and soundly financed. However, your policy may be different.

✓ Do remember that insurance may force you to improve your records and systems. This is usually a benefit.

✓ Do seriously consider credit insurance if a bad debt would have a serious effect on your business. Insurance is probably important if your business is small and/or badly financed.

✓ Do consider that very many assets and risks are routinely insured. If them, why not trade debtors too?

✓ Do not forget that you will probably not be allowed to 'cherry pick' the accounts to be insured.

✓ Do not forget that there will always be an excess on the policy. You must always bear at least a small part of the risk.

✓ Do remember that it is a competitive business. It may pay to shop around.

✓ Do consider that it may pay to insure export accounts. A whole range of political factors may be insured as well as insolvency.

✓ Do remember that the cost may well be between 0.3% of turnover and 0.7% of turnover.

✓ Do not treat credit insurance as a substitute for credit control. Even insured bad debts still carry some cost.

chapter thirteen

Less usual
chasing methods

Introduction

The great majority of businesses start the collecting process by sending out statements. There is a view that time and money should be saved by dispensing with statements as some customers disregard them. It is certainly true that some will be disregarded, but I am firmly of the opinion that statements should usually be sent. Many customers do use them for a detailed reconciliation, they act as the first reminder and the benefits of sending them outweigh the costs.

After the statements, the most common collection methods are letters or telephone calls, or a combination of the two. Standard letters are almost inevitable when a large number of small debts have to be collected. Telephone collection is especially effective, but constraints of time inevitably restrict its use. When the ledger consists of a small number of large debts it is probably possible and desirable to ring each customer as necessary. This certainly gets very good results.

After the failure of letters and telephone calls, or after an acceptable period of time has elapsed, it is usual to move on to enforcement. This usually means suspending deliveries or services (if orders are still being placed), issuing a final warning letter, then the ultimate step of taking legal action.

There are very good reasons for these being the most commonly used collection methods. They work in the great majority of cases and that is why a significant part of this Guide is devoted to them. However, it is worth a brief look at some other methods and this chapter puts some forward for consideration. Some are rather light-hearted but light-hearted methods can work, and they may trigger some useful ideas.

Methods

Personal visits

Personal visits are expensive and time-consuming. Unless you have just a few large accounts it is necessary to be very selective with the visits and to make each one effective. They are so potent that it is usually worth taking every opportunity that presents itself.

They are normally the most effective collection method of all as they put psychological pressure on the customer. It is more difficult to make excuses when there is a living person in the same room and some excuses just cannot be made. It is difficult to say that there is no one to sign a cheque when the appropriate cars are in the car park and can be seen from the office window. Other excuses can still be made but you are more likely to recognise them for what they are.

There are advantages in just dropping in, but it is usually best to say in advance that you are coming. This gives the customer time to get the cheque ready and to prepare any matters that he wants to raise. It does give him time to prepare the excuses, but this factor is usually outweighed by the advantages.

Advance notice can, at one extreme, mean a formal appointment with an agenda and a letter in advance requesting a cheque for a specified amount. At the other extreme it can be a telephone call saying that you will be dropping by in a few minute's time. Personal visits are so effective that you should maximise opportunities to make them. If you plan to drive past the end of the customer's road it may be worth finding the extra half hour needed to call in.

An often forgotten benefit of a personal visit is the saving of one or two day's interest due to the post. This is particularly valuable if the amount is large and the caller takes a bank paying-in book with him. In Chapter 1 it was pointed out that a day's interest is probably worth between 30 pence per thousand pounds per day and 45 pence per thousand pounds per day.

There are different views about asking salesmen to collect money. Advantages are:

- They are the people who frequently visit customers.

- They may be the only people able to collect on a large scale.

On the other hand, there may be very real disadvantages:

- Salesmen are employed to sell and few things should detract from this overriding objective.

- Salesmen are trained to sell, not to collect money. They may not be very good at it.

- Salesmen's contacts are usually with the buyers, not with the accounts department.

- Salesmen may dislike collecting and not be very good at it. They may resent it if it takes away time in which to earn commission.

- Salesmen may be too ready to accept customers' excuses.

This is quite a formidable list and it accounts for the fact that, in most organisations, salesmen do not regularly collect. It is difficult to generalise. Some salesmen are very good at it but others are terrible.

I strongly recommend cultivating an atmosphere where all staff visiting a customer look out for an opportunity to bring back a cheque. This does not mean that it has to be the overriding priority, just that everyone is aware that their best efforts would be appreciated. A word in the right ear can do wonders. Maybe a joke can be made of it. Perhaps the visitor can say something like 'They won't let me back in if I have not got a cheque with me. They're going to board up my office and leave me in the corridor'.

There are often opportunities for an accounts department to ask in advance for a cheque to be ready for a salesmen or other caller to collect. This takes the pressure off the salesman in that he just has to say that he believes that there is something for collection, and does not have to do any detailed negotiating. Many of the benefits of personal visits will accrue, and the customer should feel an obligation to have a cheque ready.

EDI

This stands for Electronic Data Interchange. As the name implies it is a process of linking two computers. All sorts of information may be transmitted in this way, but in the context of credit control we are most interested in linking the invoicing and sales ledger accounting of the seller with the purchase ledger accounting of the buyer. This means that an invoice is raised simultaneously in the offices of the buyer and seller. Subject to appropriate checks it is then entered into the purchase ledger of the buyer. This cuts out postal delays and the simultaneous matching of information simplifies checking and accounting.

EDI should aid the credit control effort. The purchaser is unlikely to allow you to take the money directly from him without his say so, even though it may be technically possible. It is possible that he will allow you to take it subject to his checks and approval. At the least the increased efficiency should make it easier to get payment.

EDI is expanding and you are most likely to encounter it when dealing with a large customer using highly developed systems. Increasingly this type of customer is requesting or requiring suppliers to cooperate in this field.

Fax

Fax machines are now available in very many offices. They have largely supplanted telex machines, although the latter are still found. Fax machines enable you to copy a document (such as an invoice) directly to a customer and also to transmit a letter or message in a few seconds.

When fax machines were rare they had a novelty value, and a fax message could have great psychological impact. They would often be brought directly to the desk of the addressee and meetings would even be interrupted. This now very rarely happens. As the volume of fax messages increases the seeming importance of each one diminishes. Fax owners complain of their equipment being cluttered up by unsolicited advertising.

I recommend the intelligent use of fax to send credit control messages. They may not go to the top of the pile, but they probably will not go to the bottom either. It saves at least a day's time and you can be sure that it has arrived in the customer's office. Unlike a telephone call, the message is put into print and a permanent record is issued.

Fax machines are particularly valuable for transmitting copy documents. They should always be used (when available) to send copies of missing invoices, orders, delivery notes, etc. This really does enable you to overcome one of the most commonly used excuses for delaying payment.

Customs and Excise officially require that a VAT invoice should be an original copy, or if faxed should be certified by a signature as a true copy of the original. Although this is the official position it need not worry us unduly, and I speak from personal experience. A fax copy is likely to be accepted in practice. If it is ever challenged a certified copy can always be obtained later.

The use of humour

Many years ago I was responsible for a rather ineffective purchase ledger department. There was no deliberate policy of delaying payments to suppliers, but due to inefficiency it quite often happened. One day I received a personal letter from a supplier asking me to sort out the problems on his account. The envelope contained two copies of the same letter. One was marked 'For the attention of the left hand' and the other was marked 'For the attention of the right hand'.

My first reaction was to fall about laughing, and the second was to feel embarrassed that anyone could show me up in that way. I did immediately sort out the account and a cheque for the correct amount was posted that night. It was a high risk strategy because it might have offended me and made an enemy, but the use of humour achieved the desired effect.

You may well be able to tell a funny story like the above, and you will almost certainly be aware that a humorous touch can sometimes unlock doors that normal systems do not breach. Official jokes are a contradiction in terms but you should keep in mind the potential of humour. Of course there are more opportunities if you get to know the customers. You will get to know who is likely to respond, and who is best treated in a serious manner.

When a customer sends an unexpectedly small cheque you could ring and thank him for the down payment. I did this recently and a cheque for the remainder was posted the same day. I knew the customer and he saw the joke and the point behind it. This is an example of the effective use of humour.

Publicity

All businesses fear bad publicity. Press reports of things such as safety pins in the baby food can and do cost the manufacturers vast amounts of money. This is true whether the safety pins were put there accidentally, deliberately, or even not at all.

The threat of publicity may provoke a slow payer into improving his record. It will obviously jeopardize the chance of future business and probably end such business. It is such a powerful weapon that one should consider very carefully whether one is morally justified in using it. One should also of course consider whether one is legally justified in using it and your attention is drawn to the section on harassment at the end of this chapter. Finally, it is wise to be sure that you have nothing to lose from bad publicity directed in return.

I first thought deeply about publicity when I worked for a subsidiary of Lord Grade's Associated Communications Corporation Ltd. At the Annual General Meeting a shareholder asked why Ivor Novello's bust had been removed from the foyer of the London Palladium, and asked that it be found and returned. The press took up the story and the resulting hullabaloo forced out the stories that the company had hoped to promote as a result of the meeting. The *London Evening Standard* ran the headline 'Who took Ivor's bust?'

A more vicious example of the same thing occurred at the 1991 Annual General Meeting of the Midland Bank. A shareholder compared the Chairman's salary with that of General Norman Schwarzkopf who had just led the victorious forces in the Gulf War. The press took up the story.

I think I can guarantee that a public company would consider its position carefully if it received notice that a small supplier had bought a few shares and intended to ask the following question at the Annual General Meeting:

> '*Would Sir Wilfred please accept the congratulations of shareholders on his appointment as Chairman of the Government Committee to examine the difficulties of small businesses in Wales. Would Sir Wilfred please explain why his company has delayed for over six months paying £15,000 due to David Lloyd Evans Ltd, resulting in two redundancies in that small Welsh company.*'

Businesses genuinely fear such things as letters to the local paper and approaches from television consumer programmes.

Stickers

These are either serious or humorous messages stuck on statements or other documents to increase their impact. I am very sceptical about their effectiveness but I stop short of saying that they have no effect at all. A simple message might say something like 'Overdue – Please Remit'.

They are not likely to have much influence on a large company but just might make some difference to a small customer. They might make your statements stand out from the pile.

Direct debits and standing orders

A standing order is initiated by the payer's bank. A direct debit is initiated by the beneficiary who claims payment from the payer's bank. Direct debits may be fixed amounts or for variable amounts. Direct debits may only be used by organisations authorised to do so by the banks and of course the authority of the customer to be debited must also be obtained.

Standing orders and especially direct debits are very attractive payment methods for suppliers. It is more difficult to see why customers should agree to make payment in this way and I tend to resist when asked to do so.

A reason for doing so is because the supplier may give an inducement. One example is local authorities which permit payment of rates over a period if payment is by this method. Insurance companies often allow payment by installments if this method is used.

The advantages for the seller are great and it is worth considerable efforts to persuade customers to use the system. It may be worth inducements to get them to do so. Sellers in a very strong position sometimes use force majeure to get customers to do it. Effectively customers are told that they must pay in this way or not deal at all. This might seem hard but as an adviser on credit control I cannot blame suppliers for exploiting the strength that they have.

Bank transfers

One tends to think of bank transfers as a way of remitting money overseas, and of course they are used for this purpose. However, the CHAPS system achieves same day transfer of cleared funds within this country. Again, there are obvious advantages for suppliers and I recommend that you ask for it in appropriate circumstances. If is often used where payment of cleared funds is required before goods are released. The supply of motor cars is a common example. It is very widely demanded by solicitors involved in the sale of property.

Credit cards

One thinks of credit cards in relation to the general public but there is no reason why sales to businesses should not use them. Individual businessmen carry credit cards and are capable of using them for company purchases. This is particularly true of cards such as American Express where there are high limits or no limits.

An acquaintance of mine exports services and makes a lot of semi-cold calls in foreign countries. He gets most of his payments in this way, finding the sureness and convenience well worth the percentage that he pays to the credit card companies.

Blacklisting

Earlier in this book I posed the question 'What are your sanctions?' In most cases the answer is suspension of supplies followed by legal action. A threat or the actuality of appropriate blacklisting can be very effective indeed. A formal or informal pooling of information by suppliers within the same trade has great benefits for them all. This is often done through the medium of a Trade Association. The threat of inclusion in the blacklist may persuade a customer to be reasonable.

Consideration under this heading can also be given to a threat to report the customer to his own professional organisation or trade association. The effectiveness of this will vary according to the customer, the trade, and the standards of the professional association or trade association.

Elsewhere in this book I told of a threat to report a slow paying solicitor to the Law Society. I rather suspect that the Law Society would not have helped but the threat alone achieved the desired result.

Harassment

I finish the chapter with this because you must not do it, and you may get into severe trouble if you do. Like most people, I am glad that laws exist to prevent partners and children of debtors being shamed more than is going to happen anyway. I am glad that laws exist to enforce certain standards, and to give sanctuary in a private home. Nevertheless, I sometimes feel a certain sympathy for potential harassers. There are a number of crooks who exploit suppliers, sometimes small businesses who can ill afford to lose the money. In these circumstances a series of telephone calls at 3 am can be very tempting. But do not do it please.

There is a line that must not be crossed. Various Acts of Parliament make it illegal, particularly the Administration of Justice Act 1970. So please take all the legal steps explained in this book, and stop short of anything illegal.

Checklist

✓   Do remember that in most cases statements are sent, followed by letters, telephone calls or both. If these fail, sanctions are applied. There is a good reason for this – these methods usually work.

✓   Do remember that personal visits are usually the most successful of all collection methods.

✓   Do realise, though, that personal visits are expensive and time-consuming. So you have to make each one count.

✓   Do realise that it is good to drop in on a customer unexpectedly, but it is usually even better to say in advance that you are going.

✓   Do carry a bank paying-in book with you.

✓   Do consider asking customers to have a cheque ready for collection by a salesman. This gets many of the advantages, and minimises the disadvantages, of asking salesmen to collect.

✓   Do use the fax, especially for sending copy invoices and other documents. It speeds up the sorting out of queries.

✓   Do remember that humour can be very effective.

✓   Do realise that all businesses dread bad publicity. But be careful. Read the warnings in this chapter.

✓   Do realise that stickers are probably not very effective. But they are very cheap, and might make some difference.

✓   Do remember that standing orders are very good if you can get them. Direct debits are even better. It might even be worth giving customers an inducement to use them.

✓   Do be aware of the possibilities of same-day transfer of cleared funds.

✓   Do consider blacklisting. It can be potent for some customers.

✓   Do be aware that harassment is a serious offence. Read the warnings in this chapter and do not do it.

chapter fourteen

Warning signs – danger imminent

Introduction

You will probably have seen humorous lists of danger signs. They tend to be along the lines of fountains in the entrance hall, new offices for the accounts staff and personalised number plates on the Chairman's Rolls Royce. These lists are usually highly entertaining and, although they should not be taken too seriously, they often contain a core of truth.

The points are usually based on expenditure above the means of the company, diversification away from the core business that made the company successful, and management concentrating on matters other than the direct running of the business. The corporate graveyard is full of companies whose Chief Executives received too many awards and served on too many committees.

Humorous indications apart, it is obviously extremely important that you get warning of an impending disaster. You may be able to limit or perhaps even eliminate your exposure. It may be a competitive situation and by putting on pressure you may get paid instead of someone else. This may be sad, but good business practice.

The following is a practical list designed to trigger alarm bells. In my experience the first three are the most important, and rank in the order listed.

Danger signs

A change for the worse in the payment pattern

This is the key sign. As well as a bad payments record, you are looking for a deteriorating payments record. A customer paying in 90 days instead of the usual 60 is more worrying than one who has always taken 90 days and still does. This cannot be hidden as the information is always available in the sales ledger.

Something in the voice

This may seem too intangible to rank number two on the list of warning signs. However, it has frequently alerted me to a problem and many experienced collectors would say the same.

It is very hard to describe, but you will know what is meant. It is an unusual inflection of the voice, apparent nervousness, and so on. Often it appears in the form of extra formality. It will be most readily noticed when you are familiar with the speaker and have spoken to him or her many times.

It might be termed information gleaned from a sixth sense. You should definitely trust your instincts; at least trust them as far as making further checks and being careful.

Credit agencies

Credit agencies may provide factual information, may provide opinions on individual customers, and may provide ratings according to a system (for example, A equals excellent risk, E equals poor risk, and so on).

Obviously, this is a valuable source of information and it is covered fully in Chapter 10. You may have a policy of only seeking an opinion when an account is opened, or when you have particular cause for concern. This may be understandable because of the cost and a scatter-gun approach will certainly not be economic. However, you will not get warning of a problem that is known to the credit agency but not to you.

A solution may be some sort of fail-safe system where you are automatically advised of a change in material facts, or changes in a rating. Many agencies operate such systems. It is, of course, often a good idea to seek a credit agency's opinion when you are worried by some information from another source. Also, it may be worth seeking regular opinions on certain very large accounts, even though you have no cause for concern.

Published accounts

All companies have to file accounts at Companies House. If turnover is in excess of £350,000 a full statutory audit is required. Below this figure an independent accountant's report is required. No accountant's reports are required for companies with a very small turnover. Copies of the accounts may be obtained from Companies House, either in person, or by post or, more commonly, by using the services of an agent. You could of course ask the company directly for a copy. However, you probably would not want to do this and may well not get a favourable response if you did.

A financially sophisticated person will be able to study the accounts and draw conclusions.

Great claims are made for various systems that are designed to predict company failure. Perhaps the most notable of these is the one known as the Z Score. The systems usually allocate points for various ratios in the accounts and compare accounts over several periods. Points are awarded for improvement or deterioration between the periods. The final score is compared with a pre-set scale of what is satisfactory, what is unsatisfactory and what is worrying. It is claimed that some of these systems have had remarkable success in analysing the accounts of companies that subsequently failed.

There are two significant disadvantages to the use of published accounts:

- Accounting conventions etc, may make the figures hard to interpret.

- The information is always out-of-date. A public company must file accounts within seven months of the balance sheet date. A private company must file accounts within ten months of the balance sheet date. Even if they are filed promptly, you will be studying historical information.

The obligation to publish accounts only applies to limited companies. There is no such obligation for sole traders and partnerships.

Late accounts

Financial journalists have come to be wary when publication of results is delayed, whatever the stated reason. More often than not, the figures will be bad when they are eventually published.

This has been my experience too. Good news arrives quickly. Bad news dawdles on the way.

Creative accountancy

An examination of back accounts of companies that have failed often reveals that the directors have resorted to creative accountancy. Sometimes it has been plain misleading accountancy, and occasionally downright dishonest accountancy.

Creative accountancy is not usually illegal. Auditors sometimes accept the practices, and say that the accounts give a true and fair view, but ensure that the reader has the benefit of a note to the accounts explaining what has happened. Unfortunately the notes may be obscure and only meaningful to the financially sophisticated. Quite often it is only the headline figures that make an impact.

Examples of creative accountancy are the unreasonable capitalisation of Research and Development costs, and the unreasonable capitalisation of interest in building or construction contracts. A well known instance was the practice of Pergamon Press Ltd in the 1960s. The company sold encyclopaedias in Africa and took the profits as soon as orders were taken. In practice many of the orders were later cancelled. It would have been correct to take the profits (subject to a prudent bad debt reserve) only on delivery.

Press comment

The laws of libel make it difficult for the press to voice their suspicions openly. Instead they often draw their readers' attention to impending problems in a sort of code. You may see one particular name appear frequently in articles about business problems. The text does not link the name with the problem, but nevertheless it is in the same article.

You cannot really have a policy of checking the press. There is just so much of it relative to the information to be found. However, if you stumble across something interesting you should consider the implications.

Do not always believe the press when they are wise after the event. They often claim that they 'knew' about an impending scandal and alerted their readers to it. Sometimes this is just wishful thinking and a study of back issues does not support the claim.

Following is a quotation from my book *Successful Credit Control* published by Hawksmere in 1992:

> '*At the time of writing, alert newspaper readers are noticing coded messages about a major British company. Credit Controllers might do well to ponder the implications and look to their defences.*'

I actually wrote the words in 1991. I did not feel able to say so, but I was referring to the business empire of the late Mr Robert Maxwell.

Mistakes on cheques

Hercule Poirot said that one mistake is a mistake but that two mistakes are a clue. To err is human but to do it again is suspicious.

You will be familiar with tiresome customers who forget to sign cheques or who send cheques with differing words and figures. It may be an accident, but it may be a ploy to gain time. The motive may be to save interest, but it may be that the customer is having difficulties and that funds are not available. You should consider this possibility if it happens an unreasonable number of times.

Always referred to someone else

Most people hate telling lies, especially if it is to a person that they know and like. In particular the junior staff may feel, probably correctly, that the problem is not their fault, so why should they cover up for the boss. Rather than do so they may keep referring a call to each other, or a senior person who never seems to be there.

If you keep being passed from person to person there may be bad news at the end of it. This point is very similar to 'Something in the voice'. They often go together.

People never ring back

This is similar to the heading above, especially if it is a person who is normally helpful. It is often the change in behaviour that is significant.

Cheque just never comes

You will have heard numerous times that a cheque is in the post, or that a cheque is ready and will be sent now. Then somehow it does not arrive. If it does eventually come the postmark on the envelope discloses that it was posted much later than had been said. It may be an unethical attempt to save interest, but it may happen because the customer is having a problem finding the money.

People avoiding you

People do spend a considerable time in meetings so there may be some truth in what is said, but only up to a point.

Avoiding speaking to a person, asking for payment is a classic sign of trouble. It is a way of buying time.

High staff turnover

A business that is having a problem paying its bills may be frequently replacing staff. This is because the working atmosphere is probably not happy, and because insiders want to secure their futures.

Empty shelves

This may happen when other suppliers are refusing deliveries and it is a very bad sign. It will mean less bills to pay, but even less future revenue which will make the problem worse.

It could, of course, have an innocent explanation. Perhaps it is caused by a drive to cut down surplus stocks and eliminate unprofitable lines. Perhaps it is caused by seasonal factors.

Unnaturally large orders

Large orders are usually good news. Very large orders from a customer who may have problems could be very bad news indeed. If you are unlucky and careless you may have a large bad debt, your normal business plus the extra orders as well.

It is worth considering if your customer has increased his order to you because he cannot get supplies elsewhere.

Round sum cheques

Round sum cheques may be sent because of staff problems, or because of problems reconciling the account, or because of an attempt to make a fair payment pending resolution of a dispute. On the other hand, a round sum cheque may be sent because money is short and the full exact sum cannot be found.

You should, of course, take and bank a round sum cheque, because it is better than nothing. But do consider the possible implications.

None of the above points should be taken as proof that serious trouble is pending. An innocent explanation is always possible. However, you should take them seriously, and if you notice two or more, you should be even more cautious.

Checklist

✓ Do remember that the most compelling sign is often a change for the worse in the pattern of payments. A change for the worse is often more worrying than a consistently bad performance.

✓ Do remember that a change in attitude by a customer (something in the voice) is a telling sign.

✓ Do remember that credit agencies are professionals who may give you good warning.

✓ Do trust your intuition, at least as far as making further enquiries. It is frequently very reliable.

✓ Do realise that published accounts are always out-of-date.

✓ Do keep in mind that creative accountancy and late accounts are often bad signs.

✓ Do worry if you spot a warning (often disguised) in the press.

✓ Do worry if a customer makes repeated mistakes on cheques sent to you.

✓ Do be concerned if you experience a change in behaviour. Examples may be normally helpful people becoming unhelpful, normally communicative people becoming hard to contact, and people never returning calls and being forever in meetings.

✓ Do pause for a moment's thought if you receive an unnaturally large order.

✓ Do realise that a round sum payment on an account is an obvious indication of possible problems.

✓ Do consider using a credit agency to double check if you are worried.

✓ Do remember that all warning signs may have an innocent explanation. It is more worrying when the warning signs are several and from different sources.

chapter fifteen

Conditions of sale

Introduction

Conditions of sale are rather like the fire instructions displayed in hotel bedrooms. For long periods they do not seem to matter, but when they are needed they are needed rather badly. It is worth spending some time and money to get them right, but fortunately this work does not have to be repeated too frequently. Do not forget though to look at the conditions if circumstances change.

In practice, sellers' terms do not govern the majority of contracts. This can be for one of four reasons:

- The seller does not bother with terms.

- The seller agrees to accept the buyer's terms.

- The seller does have terms but fails to try and ensure that they govern the contract.

- The seller tries to make sure that his terms govern the contract, but does not succeed in doing so.

A sale is often not governed by clear conditions. This is either because no attempt is made to agree them, or because both sides have a comprehensive set of terms which each maintains prevail over the terms of the other.

A licensed insolvency practitioner has told me that he rejects more than half of the retention of title claims made to him. In a few cases the reason was that the wording of the appropriate clause was defective and did not match the exact circumstances. However, in the great majority of cases it was because the terms did not govern the contract. Please think about this for a moment. In more than 50% of cases, carefully (and probably expensively) drawn up terms were of no use because they did not govern the contract.

The latter part of this chapter is a study of the main terms, but an essential place to start is the legal status of terms, and how to ensure that they apply.

The legal position with terms

As a seller you will want to ensure that your terms legally govern the contract, but be warned that this is not easy. It is only of very limited use printing the terms on invoices, statements, delivery documents, etc. This is because these documents are issued after the contract has been made, and what matters is what is agreed at the time that the contract is made.

It is of course a good idea to print the terms on these documents, and there may be various practical (as opposed to legal) benefits. From the legal point of view it just may help to build up the case that the terms (if unchallenged) had become custom and practice between the parties. But this is very insubstantial; what matters is what is agreed (or at least stated) at the time that the contract is made.

Sellers' terms can govern the contract because of one of the following four reasons:

- The customer has signed a specific order containing the terms, or referring to them.

- The customer has signed a document stating that the seller's terms will apply to all future business.

- The seller's terms were last on the table, even if not specifically agreed, at the time that the contract was made.

- Custom and practice can be held to show that the seller's terms apply.

Obviously points one and two are the most satisfactory. A suitably senior signature should be virtually unanswerable. It is often good practice to write to all customers, enclosing a copy of the terms, and seeking a signature to confirm that they will apply to all future business. This overcomes the need to check that all orders are actually signed and it deals with such things as telephone orders.

It is unlikely to be a problem, but you should be aware of the meaning of the term '*ostensible authority*'. It means that it is reasonable to think that the person signing has the authority to do so. It is nearly always reasonable to think that a managing director has authority to commit a buyer even if, unknown to you, the buyer's company has a rule that three directors' signatures are required. You would be on unsafe ground if a person known to be very junior signed for a very high-value purchase.

It frequently happens that the seller has a comprehensive set of terms, and so does the buyer. Each tries to make their terms govern the contract, each refuses to sign the other's form and each maintains that its own terms predominate. In these circumstances the rule is that the last terms mentioned (or on the table) when the contract was made will usually prevail. Unfortunately it can all get very childish, but it is the law and you disregard it at your peril.

What can happen is often known as the battle of the forms. For example, consider the following scenario: —

- The salesman makes a sale and at the same time hands over an order form with a copy of the seller's terms. If this is all that happens the seller's term's will apply.

- The buyer says that he will not accept the terms. At this point neither set of terms apply.

- The buyer writes to the seller confirming that he wishes to place an order and encloses a copy of his buying conditions. At this point the buyer's terms apply.

- The seller writes back thanking him for the order but pointing out that it can only be accepted if his terms apply. At this point the seller's terms apply.

- The buyer telephones and tells the seller not to be silly. He insists that his terms apply and if they want the order, they had better let the matter drop. At this point the buyer's terms apply.

- The seller delivers the goods and one day later writes to say that he only did so on the understanding that his terms apply. This is no good as he is only doing so after 'offer and acceptance'. The buyer's terms will apply.

This is all very silly. If the participants were children they would undoubtedly be sent to bed without any supper. But it is the law and you should be aware of it.

If there is no agreement it may be possible to establish that certain terms apply because of 'custom and practice'. Every bit of evidence helps. Among the things considered could be:

- Accepted practice within the industry.

- Terms on which previous business between the parties had been conducted.

- The seller's standard terms which have been repeatedly seen by the buyer. This could be because they are printed on invoices and statements. It is weak, but better than nothing, and may reinforce other evidence.

Most of the remainder of this chapter studies individual conditions of sale. Before considering these though, do be fully aware of the details of this section. It is no good having absolutely ideal terms if they do not apply.

Display of conditions of sale

Conditions of sale are often long and technical. Partly for this reason they are often printed in small print on the reverse side of documents. Admittedly, another reason may be that the seller does not want them studied. This is fine so long as the buyer's attention is drawn to them. A prominent sentence on the front stating that the terms are on the back will usually have the desired legal effect.

You may well not want the terms studied closely, but there is usually at least one exception. You should want the buyer to know and accept the period of credit. This can be achieved by a prominent statement on the front similar to the following:

> *'All invoices are payable on the last day of the month following the date of the invoice. Terms and conditions are on the back of this order.'*

The terms

Alternative approaches to terms

You may decide on a short, fair, simple statement of the main terms. This will probably be good for customer relations and, because it can be seen to be fair, is more likely to be accepted by the customer.

On the other hand you may decide on the opposite. This is terms that are long, unfair and complicated, and written with the intention of giving you every conceivable advantage. Terms of this sort are less likely to be accepted by customers.

The second sort of terms (if accepted by customers) are likely to give you much better protection. This is presumably the reason why they are much more common. I tend to prefer the first sort, even as a seller acting in my own best interest, but this is obviously not a generally accepted viewpoint. The exact balance depends on individual circumstances and individual judgment.

Drawing up the terms

You could write the conditions yourself, or more realistically you could copy someone else's. Both approaches are probably a mistake. You are very likely not to get it completely right if you do it yourself. Someone else's terms may be defective, may not be up-to-date, may not be comprehensive and may not exactly match your circumstances. Some points, such as retention of title clauses, are inevitably rather technical.

It is normally essential that a solicitor draws up the terms. Make sure that the solicitor gives you exactly what you want and does not take on a momentum of his own. Good solicitors understand the commercial realities and welcome firm guidance. Some, though, may give you technically sound terms that are impossibly complicated, or in some other way may not be what you want.

Conditions of sale are partly driven by legal considerations and partly by commercial judgment. The solicitor will supply the legal part and you should exercise the commercial judgment. If you do disregard the solicitor's advice you should, or course, realise that you may be lessening your protection.

Advice to buyers

This Guide gives advice to sellers, but many readers will sometimes be in the position of buyers as well. This very small section is advice for them.

Sellers' conditions of sale are frequently ridiculously unfair and indefensible. If this is the case do not put up with it. Put a line through them, or delete the clauses that you consider to be unfair. It never ceases to amaze me how many buyers do sign monstrously unfair conditions. More often than not the seller is bluffing and his bluff should be called.

I was once asked to sign terms that stated that any damage to goods in transit, and prior to delivery, would be the responsibility of the buyer (me). This remarkable provision was buried deep in the middle of a minutely printed four page document. I rang the managing director and promised 60 seconds total silence whilst he explained to me why I should sign it. We both laughed and he agreed that I should strike it out, as he would have done.

The main terms affecting credit control

The remainder of this chapter consists of a review of the main terms affecting credit control:

Period of credit

This is probably the most important of all the conditions, and it is important because it always matters. Most of the other conditions are theoretical and are only referred to when there is a problem. The period of credit is not like that. It is always important and it affects every single sale.

You want the customer to know and accept the period of credit. It is good for it to have legal validity but this is not enough. You want the customer to know it. For this reason it should not just be included in the small print on the back of the documents. This one should go prominently on the front. It normally is not longer than one sentence.

Even if you do not bother with conditions of sale, this one should be the exception. It is always important.

You will want the period of credit to be as short as possible, but you will be influenced by the attitude of competitors, tradition in the industry, etc. It is wonderful to be a monopoly supplier or a near-monopoly supplier, but we live in very competitive times and very few of us are in that position. The liquidity and attitude of the customer must also be taken into account. The more that he wants extended credit, the more he may be willing to concede on other matters, such as price.

It is worth repeating the advice given in Chapter 3. There are three cynical but practical reasons for making the nominal period of credit as short as possible:

- A very few customers will pay to terms, whatever they are. Believe it or not there are still one or two who will, unprompted, respond to seven day terms by posting a cheque on the sixth day. Admittedly, they may not operate in your sector. A slightly larger group will, unprompted, pay just after the nominally due date.

- Quite a large group of customers will take a fixed time beyond the nominal date, whatever it is. They have, for example, a cynical policy of taking an extra 30 days. If you specify 7 days you will be paid after 37 days. If you say 30 days you will be paid after 60 days. If you say six months then seven months will be taken.

- Your collection procedures will be geared to the nominal due date and normally only start at this point. If you have an extended nominal period of credit then you are starting collecting late.

You should carefully consider the difference between a fixed number of days after invoice date and terms such as 'net monthly account'. They are sometimes wrongly taken to mean much the same thing. An invoice issued on April 8th, with 30 days terms, is due for payment on May 8th. The same invoice with 'net monthly account' is due at the end of the following month, namely May 31st. Monthly account gives an average of 15 days more than 30 day terms.

The Late Payment of Commercial Debts (Interest) Act 1998 provides for statutory interest to start after 30 days. This period can be overturned by a contract, but only if the contract provides a 'substantial remedy'. You should be aware of the 30 day period stipulated by the Act.

Retention of title

This is sometimes known as the Romalpa Clause after the legal case of that name. Without retention of title, ownership normally passes to the buyer on delivery. If there is a retention of title clause in the conditions, ownership is normally retained by the seller until payment is complete.

Retention of title clauses are usually fairly technical, which is one reason why they should normally be drafted by a solicitor. Circumstances vary and the solicitor will probably try to give you the maximum rights possible. For example, you will often only be able to repossess specific goods listed on an unpaid invoice. However, the solicitor may endeavour to give you the right to repossess all goods so long as just one invoice is overdue and unpaid.

Retention of title means that you can get back the goods if you are having a problem getting payment. It is most often used in the case of a liquidation, where the return of the goods is worth more than (if you are lucky) x pence in the pound. If there is a liquidation, make your retention of title claim quickly and vigorously. You should do this before stock goes missing.

Liquidators are professional people who know the law. They will make you prove that the retention of title clause applies, and they will make you prove that it was agreed as part of the contract. Many suppliers fall at this hurdle and your attention is drawn to the earlier part of this chapter.

Retention of title is not always the panacea that is sometimes supposed. There are several important provisos:

- Your rights are only against your own customer. You cannot normally extend them to a third party who has bought the goods in good faith.

- By definition, it is only possible to repossess goods, not services. It is normally of no value to a management consultant or a comedian who has not been paid for a performance.

- You cannot repossess goods that have been altered by your customer. For example, if you supply leather you can only repossess the leather, not shoes that have been made out of that leather.

- You must give full credit for the items that you take back. You cannot say that the goods are not worth so much because they are old stock or the fashion has changed. You can, of course, say it, but you must still give full credit.

- You will be responsible for the transport costs.

- You can only get the goods back with the customer's agreement or with a court order. You do not have the right of forcible entry.

- According to the exact wording of the clause, you can normally only repossess items identified as unpaid, not all items of yours that the customer still has. If a customer has paid some invoices but not others, you are only allowed to take items listed on the unpaid invoices. However, the exact wording may give you this right.

- You must be able to identify the goods as yours. This is often obvious, but in some cases it can be difficult.

Two of the above problems are well illustrated by a supplier of screws. The customer tipped all screws of a certain size into a large hopper. This hopper contained screws from two different manufacturers, and it contained some screws which had been paid for and some screws which had not been paid for. In these circumstances, repossession was in practice not possible.

Repossession, and enforcement of retention of title can be a big administrative task. It is a task in which, understandably, the customer may be unwilling to assist. You must make precise records of what you take, give the customer a copy, then raise an accurate credit note based on the records.

One of the provisos is that you can only get back the goods with the customer's agreement, or with a court order. In fact it is very common to bluff on this point; to just turn up and say that you have come to collect the goods. A very sad and shell shocked customer will usually let you do it. However, this does not always work, and is most unlikely to work with a liquidator.

In practice it is often a matter of fine judgment whether or not a retention of title clause should be enforced. Suppose that you are owed £1,000, a liquidator has been appointed, and you expect to receive 20 pence in the pound. You will eventually (perhaps much later) receive £200. If your mark-up is 100% the goods that you repossess will, at most, only be worth £500 to you. The goods will be old, possibly soiled, possibly out of fashion and possibly in uneconomic quantities. You will have to pay for transport and administration. It may be a difficult decision to make.

All the above restrictions and limitations are very real, and they do diminish the value of retention of title. Nevertheless, retention of title can be very valuable and one of the most powerful weapons in the credit controller's armoury. You are advised to give it careful consideration.

Quantity discount

This is sometimes known as retrospective discount and is the discount given at the end of a period as a reward for the value of business placed. A typical example would be 5% of turnover over £100,000, and it can be very worthwhile for the customer.

It is desirable to make it conditional on all invoices during the period being paid in accordance with agreed terms. It can be very effective to ring a customer towards the end of the year and point out that late payment is putting at risk the credit note for a whole year's quantity discount.

Settlement discount

This means that the customer deducts a certain sum or percentage for paying by a certain date. A typical example would be 'payable after 30 days, or 5% settlement for payment within 7 days'.

There are obvious advantages and it can be a powerful incentive to get customers to pay promptly. It is often used when money is in short supply and it is worth paying a high price to get the debts paid. Settlement discount is often most effective when first introduced and it can give a kick start to the cash flow. It has to be tightly policed in order to be effective. Unfortunately there are very definite drawbacks:

- Some customers might have paid on time anyway. They get the benefit for nothing.

- It is usually expensive. In the above example 5% is being given for 23 days, which is equal to 79% per year.

- Once introduced it may be difficult to withdraw.

- It requires extra effort to monitor.

- There is always the tendency for the customer to take the discount without paying within the permitted time. There will be difficult decisions and many arguments, both with the customer and within the selling organisation. Customers will cite alleged delivery problems as a reason for paying late and still taking the settlement discount. Sales directors will shout 'Are you really going to crucify my sales just for six miserable days?'

Settlement discount is traditional and extremely common in some trades. Customers in these trades may expect it and may even try to take it although it has not been offered. In these circumstances it can be politic to give settlement discount but adjust prices to compensate.

Interest

The Late Payment of Commercial Debts (Interest) Act 1998 is now law. This provides for statutory interest and takes effect in three stages. Subject to the stages, interest may be claimed in one of three circumstances:

- If it is provided for in the terms governing a contract.

- If legal action is taken and judgment obtained. In this case interest at the statutory rate may be enforced.

- Statutory interest under the Late Payment of Commercial Debts (Interest) Act 1998.

Despite statutory interest, there are advantages to including interest in the conditions of sale. It is still not common, and it is even less common for it to be actually enforced and obtained. Commercial considerations are responsible for this, as a claim for interest will usually antagonise a late-paying customer. The fact that the customer has behaved unfairly, and the supplier has suffered, will rarely in practice make any difference. The customer will feel aggrieved.

Customers in a strong position may well not agree to terms stipulating the payment of interest, and they may not pay it even if it is in the terms. The problem is most acute when a small supplier deals with a large customer. I regret that I cannot offer anything except sympathy. The commercial realities have to be a matter for you.

I can recommend trying to get interest included in the terms and conditions. It does after all seem only fair. If it is included you can make a case by case decision about whether to try and enforce it. Even if commercial realities dictate that it is not normally enforced, there are two circumstances where it almost certainly should be:

- When a customer has ceased trading with you, and there is little or no prospect of more business. In this case there is usually nothing to lose by getting what you can.

- When a customer has gone into liquidation and is paying x pence in the pound. The same thing applies and by claiming interest you should get a percentage of a bigger figure.

Interest can usually be claimed over a period of six years until it becomes statute barred. So a failure to collect it at the time does not prevent you claiming later. This can be a very nasty shock for a customer that has gone into liquidation or behaved in an unfair manner. Interest on all late payments, over several years, may add up to a significant sum. If you do get it, it is almost 100% profit contribution.

Full details of the Late Payment of Commercial Debts (Interest) Act 1998 are given in Appendix A to this Guide. Statutory interest is not intended to replace provision for interest in mutually agreed terms. However, it is not possible to contract out of statutory interest. Mutually agreed terms will only apply if they provide a 'substantial remedy'. If they do not do so, the Act will override the mutually agreed terms.

The Act provides for interest of 8% over base rate and the interest starts to run after 30 days. Enforcement of statutory interest is not compulsory, which would in any case be impossible. Suppliers may choose to enforce it or they may choose not to enforce it.

Statutory interest takes effect in three stages:

- Contracts made from 1st November 1998 – small businesses against large enterprises and the public sector.

- Contracts made from 1st November 2000 – small businesses against all enterprises and the public sector.

- Contracts made from 1st November 2002 – all businesses and the public sector against all businesses and the public sector.

Miscellaneous

There are hundreds of other items that might be considered for inclusion in the conditions of sale. Each reader must compile his or her own list, but it might include a minimum order size and the method of payment. For export sales you might for example want to specify payment in sterling to a UK bank.

An important point reiterated

You may have absolutely superb terms. But they will be of no use if they do not govern the contract. It is a common failing.

Checklist

✓ Do realise that the seller's conditions of sale only govern the contract if they are agreed (or at least last on the table) when the contract is made. Producing them afterwards will not do.

✓ Do realise that, in the majority of cases, sellers' conditions of sale do not govern the contract. Resolve not to be part of that unfortunate majority.

✓ Do think about '*the battle of the forms*'. Detailed notes are in this chapter.

✓ Do get a solicitor to draft the conditions of sale, but do stay in charge. It is you who should take the final decisions.

✓ When you are a buyer, do not accept sellers' unreasonable terms. Strike them out. They can sometimes be very unreasonable indeed. The seller is often bluffing.

✓ Do remember that the nominal period of credit is always important. It should be prominent in the terms; the customer should know it and agree it.

✓ Do remember that there is a strong case for making the nominal period of credit as short as possible.

✓ Do understand that retention of title is potentially a strong weapon in your armoury. However, there are several limitations listed in this chapter.

✓ Do remember that retention of title may be particularly valuable if the customer goes into liquidation. You may have to act quickly before the stock goes missing.

✓ Do understand that settlement discount may give a boost to the cash flow. However, it is expensive and continued monitoring is essential.

✓ Do remember that it may well be worth putting interest into the conditions of sale.

✓ Do remember that you may choose not to actually claim interest, even if it is in the conditions of sale. You can claim it later if necessary.

✓ Do remember that a law provides for statutory interest. The law takes effect in stages.

✓ Do remember that statutory interest overrides a contract, unless the contract provides a 'substantial remedy'.

chapter sixteen

Legal action – considerations prior to commencement

Introduction

It is sometimes said that declaration of war is the ultimate failure of diplomacy. In the same way, legal action against a debtor signifies the end of a normal trading relationship. You will (or should) have stopped supplies. It is probable that you will not supply the same customer again. If you do so, the relationship will (or should) be a different one. You will need guarantees, or some very firm and believable assurances, that things will be different in future.

If you are about to start legal proceedings then something has gone wrong with your normal trading methods and controls. Just possibly, you need to ask some questions about what has gone wrong and why. But do not spend too much time doing this. Everyone is unlucky from time to time and most businesses run some risks in order to secure sales. Any business that has a certain number of credit accounts will inevitably, from time to time, need to consider taking legal action. If there are a large number of credit accounts, legal action or write-offs are inevitable.

Chapter 17 shows how to obtain judgment, and Chapter 18 shows how to enforce judgment and actually secure payment. This introductory chapter is very important and you will use Chapters 17 and 18 more effectively if you have studied it. It gives background information about the legal process, draws attention to points that you should consider and decisions that you should make, and shows how to effectively plan to enforce your rights.

Scottish law

Scottish law has many similarities to English law, but there are differences. You should therefore not rely on these legal chapters if you are enforcing a debt where Scottish law applies. The legal forms are, in any case, different. Much of the general advice in this chapter is equally applicable and well worth consideration.

The same advice applies to other jurisdictions outside England and Wales, such as Northern Ireland, Jersey, etc.

The significance of retention of title

Retention of title was studied in detail in Chapter 15 on conditions of sale. It also features in Chapter 20 on bad debts.

Retention of title is designed to help you in circumstances such as the ones that you are now facing. It is often not the panacea that is sometimes supposed; there are practical constraints on its use, and even if you succeed in recovering the goods, the financial benefits will be inferior to getting your invoices paid. You are recommended to refer back to Chapter 15, and study the details of the constraints and how retention of title works.

Despite the drawbacks, retention of title should be considered if it applies, and if the practical difficulties are not too great. This, of course, assumes that goods are still in the physical possession of your customer. It may well have an extremely beneficial psychological effect on the customer if he is still in business. For a start, it shows that you are serious. It may be very damaging to his business if you repossess your supplies. He might need them urgently. Also, it could be extremely bad for his reputation if word gets out, and if there are embarrassing gaps on his shelves. It may be very bad for the morale of his staff too.

Perhaps only part of the goods are in the possession of the customer. If this is the case you can repossess these (or try to) and take legal action for the balance of the debt. You must give full credit for the goods that you take back, even though they may not be worth as much to you.

Have other steps been exhausted?

The great majority of legal actions for recovery of debt are successful. That is to say, they are successful in obtaining judgment; they are by no means all successful in enforcing judgment and actually obtaining payment. The reason that they are successful is that there is no dispute about the money being owing. Everyone knows that the money is owing; it is just that the customer will not, or cannot, pay it within an acceptable time scale.

The sad reality is that, in most cases, the threat of legal action, then the reality of legal action, is what comes after the number two letter. Real disputes, as opposed to spurious disputes, are comparatively rare.

If there is a real dispute it is worth making strenuous efforts to resolve it before commencing legal proceedings. A defended legal action is very different to an uncontested one. If your action is undefended you should get judgment in a matter of weeks and can then get on with enforcing the judgment. A defended action will drag on for a long time. Certainly, several months as a minimum. Both sides will incur costs, and if you lose you will probably have to pay the costs of both sides. Even if you win you will probably not recover all that you have actually spent. A defended action will cost time as well as money and, depending on the strength of your case, there is a risk that you might lose.

For all these reasons it is probably worth trying to compromise and resolve a dispute without legal action. It might save you a customer as well. I am not advocating giving away too much, just being sensible.

Some writers on credit control advocate offering to settle for less than the full amount, even though there is no real dispute. They advocate this on purely practical grounds, saying that it is a cost effective thing to do. They say that if you are owed £1,070, a without prejudice offer to settle for an immediate £1,000 in full and final payment, will often work.

I most emphatically disagree. Why on earth should you do this? Your case is good, so you will win. Apart from moral considerations there is a very practical reason for not doing it. You cannot afford the reputation of someone who is open to this sort of settlement. It is catching. Others may try to get the same favour. It is a digression, but interesting to note that Robert Maxwell would often seek to reduce his debts by offering immediate payment of a reduced sum in full and final settlement.

Without prejudice offers

In the above section, compromise was discussed. If there is a genuine dispute it may well pay to try and negotiate a settlement. If you try to do this, you will want to make sure that your efforts do not count against you if compromise fails. You most definitely do not want your offer quoted against you in court and taken into account in the legal process.

To avoid this you should memorise the words '**WITHOUT PREJUDICE**', clearly quote them on any document concerned with the attempted settlement, and say them before any verbal offer. It works in the following way:

- All correspondence and offers should very clearly be marked '**WITHOUT PREJUDICE**'.

- No documents marked in this way can be used in the legal process.

- The other party may accept a without prejudice offer, which is the point of making it. When a without prejudice offer is accepted it becomes a contract and is binding on both parties.

- If an oral compromise is reached it is binding, but it is very sound practice to confirm the agreement in writing. This avoids arguments about exactly what was agreed.

Should you take legal action?

Legal action will cost money, very probably more than the costs that you will recover from the debtor if you win. It will also take some time, possibly not very much but in some cases a great deal of your time. This may be in filling in forms and perhaps in providing information for your solicitor or credit agent. If the case is defended the time requirement will escalate.

You should only take legal action if all other reasonable procedures have been exhausted. This means that normal, reasonable requests for payment have been made and a final warning letter has been sent. If there is a genuine dispute, there should have been a reasonable attempt to settle it.

Does the debtor have the means to pay? If he genuinely does not, then legal action is pointless. Blood cannot be got out of a stone. Obtaining judgment would turn out to be a paper victory. The object is to get actual payment.

Finally, it is sometimes necessary to ask yourself if you are proposing legal action for commercial reasons, or if you are doing it as a matter of principle. Principles are very fine things. We all should have them. But be clear about your motivation. If you are doing it on principle, and not for the money, you should acknowledge it to yourself and perhaps to the boss (if you have one).

The final warning letter

It is sad, but true, that some customers will only make payment when faced with the imminent prospect of something unpleasant, or the reality of something unpleasant. Payment is often forthcoming when customers are faced with the following:

- Supplies are cut off. This assumes that they want further supplies and cannot conveniently obtain them elsewhere.

- They receive a credible final warning of impending legal action.

- Legal action is commenced and they receive either a writ or a county court summons.

- Judgment is entered against them. Judgment is entered on the Register of county court Judgments but the entry may be removed if payment in full is made within a month.

- Enforcement proceedings are taken.

A credible final warning letter will produce payment in well over 50% of all cases. So it is very well worth issuing such a letter, and making it a good one. This was covered in detail in Chapter 6. Please note that the letter must be *credible*. It should say what is going to happen and when it is going to happen. And the customer should believe it.

A good example of a final warning letter was given in Chapter 6, and it is repeated in Appendix D at the end of this book. A good final warning letter will have the following features:

- By definition there is only one final warning letter. If you send more than one, something is wrong.

- It should not make empty threats. If you do not mean it, do not say it.

- It should be short and to the point.

- It should state the exact deadline and the amount to be paid. It is marginally better to state an exact date rather than a number of elapsed days.

- It should state exactly what will happen if payment is not made by the specified date.

In order to achieve maximum impact it is sound practice to send the final warning letter by recorded delivery. For the same reason it is a good idea, in some circumstances, to send the letter to a person who has not been involved so far, and with a copy to the original contact. If the customer is a company, it could achieve extra impact to address the letter to the Company Secretary.

Look at your conditions of sale

Some suppliers do not bother with conditions of sale, others do but fail to make them legally enforceable. If you do have enforceable conditions of sale, they may contain something that will help you in the present situation. This was explored in detail in Chapter 15.

It may be possible to raise further invoices and take legal action to recover a larger amount. Sometimes not absolutely everything permitted by the contract is actually invoiced. Examples may be certain travel and training costs. These are waived in the interests of the long-term relationship. If you are taking legal action there almost certainly is not going to be a long-term relationship. You may as well increase the amount and get what you can.

You should seriously consider invoicing for interest if permitted to do so under the terms of a contract. This may generally be done, subject to contract terms, from the dates that payments become contractually due, and it may be possible to claim interest on late payments that have been received. The amounts involved may be large. It may be done for a period back to when the claim is statute-barred. This is five years for Scotland and six years for the rest of the UK.

If contractual interest does not apply, you should seriously consider claiming statutory interest under the Late Payment of Commercial Debts (Interest) Act 1998.

Statutory interest

You may be able to claim statutory interest under the Late Payment of Commercial Debts (Interest) Act 1998. Full details of the Act are given in Appendix A. The Act takes effect in stages with the final stage taking effect for contracts made after 1st November 2002.

The Act provides for interest at 8% over base rate, so it is well worth claiming and the amounts involved may be quite large.

Unclaimed interest may be claimed right back to the time that the claim is statute-barred. This is five years for Scotland and six years for the rest of the UK. Perhaps interest has not been claimed because of customer relations. But customer relations do not now matter too much. It is time to get what you can.

Who to use

There are three possibilities:

- You can do it yourself.

- You can use a solicitor.

- You can use a credit agency.

If you use the High Court it is a requirement that a solicitor acts for a limited company. This is not the case if a county court is used and you are permitted to do the work yourself if you wish. The High Court requirement to use a solicitor does not necessarily mean a solicitor in practice. Many credit agencies employ solicitors and some large companies do so too.

To fill in the forms for the county court, and to do the other work, may seem a daunting prospect, but it is entirely feasible to do the work yourself. If you handle a significant number of cases you will become practised and proficient, and obtain the benefit of economies of scale. You will save money too.

On the other hand, we employ specialists to do a lot of things that we could do for ourselves. I am well able to clean windows, but I still employ a window cleaner to clean the office windows. This is because he is a specialist and he does it more quickly than I do. It pays me to concentrate on what I am good at and the main purpose of my business. It is a matter of individual judgment. It probably pays to use a solicitor if the case is very complicated or defended, and a company has to do so if it is a High Court action.

Legal services

Payment for legal services

Solicitors traditionally charge for their time and also for reimbursement of their expenses and court costs. Some still do charge in this way, especially if you only use their services rarely. However, many now charge a percentage of the sum actually recovered. Many credit agencies operate in this way too. The eye catching appeal is 'NO WIN – NO FEE'. They say that you have nothing to lose by engaging their services. This is not strictly true because you will almost always be responsible for court fees, whether anything is recovered or not.

It works according to the following hypothetical example:

10% of amount recovered	from 0 – £500
5% of amount recovered	from £501 – £1,000
2% of amount recovered	from £1,001 – £5,000
1% of amount recovered	over £5,000

The solicitor or credit agency is expecting a reasonable mix of large debts and small debts, and a reasonable mix of good prospects and difficult prospects. Usually the fee is payable even if payment is obtained without legal action being taken. It is normal for the solicitor or credit agency to send a warning letter and this often gets good results.

Payment by this method can be a good idea. There is considerable attraction in 'NO WIN – NO FEE'. However, do not forget the court fees which you will usually have to pay.

Do be careful if you pass over a large debt with a good chance of success. The amount of work involved in collecting a large debt may be no more than the amount of work involved in collecting a small debt. It may even be less. Under the above scale of charges you will pay £30 for the successful collection of a £300 debt. But you will pay £1,105 for the successful collection of a £100,000 debt. If you have a large debt with good prospects of success, it may pay to negotiate with the solicitor or credit agency, and ask for special terms.

Advice on using solicitors and other specialists

Books such as this often advise that, if you appoint a solicitor, you should always do what he says without question. I do not agree with this advice and neither do many solicitors. Certainly you should take your solicitor's advice on legal matters, and beware of the consequences if you do not, but the same is not necessarily the case with commercial decisions. You know most about your business and it is you who should take these decisions, after considering the advice of course.

You may decide that it is too expensive to continue, or too time consuming, or the risk of bad publicity is too great. Perhaps you come to feel sorry for the debtor. This can often happen and you will probably encounter some very sad cases. You may want your solicitor or agent to follow a different line of action or enforcement, or to take payment by installments.

Sometimes a case can take on a momentum of its own, but my advice is to stay in charge. This is not hostile to solicitors, many of whom welcome clients who wish to give firm guidance.

On a different matter, large amounts of time can be wasted preparing for legal proceedings. Remember, that the great majority of the actions will not be contested. All too often there is a reflex reaction of photocopying all outstanding invoices for the solicitor, and many other documents too. It is done because it is always done, and everyone would rather be safe than sorry. If there are only one or two invoices it will not take long, but if there are hundreds it can be an enormous job.

The solicitor has to prepare the claim, and to do this he will need a list of all outstanding invoices, showing invoice numbers, dates and amounts. He will also need to know what the invoices are for, but often a sentence or paragraph will give this information.

My advice is to give the solicitor or credit agency the above and ask if it will suffice. Very often it will suffice and you can save yourself a job. If it is especially complicated, or there are difficult features you can do it on request. Also, you can do it later if it is necessary to rebut a defence that is entered.

The costs of legal action

Many of the main court fees are set out in Appendix C. These may be recoverable from the customer if you win. But they have to be paid in advance by you. 'Recoverable from the customer' means actually paid by the customer. Judgment in your favour is not the same thing, the customer must actually hand over the money. You are, of course, taking legal action to force your customer to hand over some money, but if you fail (despite obtaining judgment), the amount to be written off will be bigger.

If the action is contested, and if you win, you will probably get your legal costs paid. The bad news is that it will be according to a scale which may well not completely cover all that you have paid out. If you lose a contested case you will probably have to pay your customer's legal costs as well as your own. In these circumstances, the miserliness (as solicitors see it) of the scale charges will work in your favour. You will probably pay less than your customer has actually spent.

You may reduce the impact of costs by using a solicitor who only charges a percentage of the sum actually recovered. Even then you will almost certainly have to pay the court costs. It may be obvious, but solicitors make a profit, even ones who only charge a percentage of the sum recovered. You pay in the end, but the successful recoveries subsidise the unsuccessful actions.

If you are doing the work yourself you will not have solicitors' costs. Do not underestimate the cost of your own time. It is a common mistake.

Taking action

To reiterate a point, do remember that if you win you must actually recover your costs from the customer. Getting judgment is not the same as actually getting paid.

All this may seem designed to stop you taking legal action. This is most definitely not the purpose, but you should be knowledgeable about the costs. Most actions are not defended and these are much cheaper than those that are. You should think about the costs if you have the prospect of a defended case.

The importance of getting key facts right

The law requires certain details to be exactly correct. In particular, it requires the defendant to be correctly identified. If you get it wrong it will probably delay your action and result in extra costs. It is not too difficult to get it wrong, so take care.

Is the defendant a sole trader, a partnership, a limited company or PLC, or is it some other body such as a building society or trade union? The first step is to get it clear in your mind; the second step is to research the details and write it down correctly.

It is a legal requirement that limited companies, and certain other bodies have to record key information on their stationery. A limited company is required to show the full and exact name of the company, the company registration number, and the address of the registered office. An offence is committed if it fails to do so. It is very sound practice to send a piece of the customer's notepaper to your solicitor or credit agent. It is a good idea to do this in all cases, not just when the customer is a company.

If the defendant is a company the documents must be addressed to the registered office. This address can be discovered, so long as the exact company name is known, but it saves a lot of trouble if you have the notepaper. There are over a million companies on the register, so it is a big index to check.

It may not be completely clear who the defendant should be. Customers do not always make it easy to know if they are acting as individuals, on behalf of a partnership, or on behalf of a limited company. Sometimes your own systems may be at fault. But it has to be right. John Brown is not the same as John Brown Ltd, and neither are the same as John Brown (Systems) Ltd.

Of course other details should be right too. You should be claiming exactly what is owing, no less and certainly no more. The details of the claim should be exactly correct.

The danger of delay

If you are having problems with a customer, it is probable that others are too. You will be in competition with other suppliers, and you may be at a disadvantage if you delay. This applies to delay in getting judgment, and it applies to steps to enforce the judgment.

It is often thought that assets seized from the debtor will be applied pro rata for the benefit of all creditors with judgments outstanding. This is not so. The money will be applied to the creditors according to the dates on which the warrants of execution were issued. The same applies to other enforcement methods.

This can be illustrated with a rather extreme example:

- ABC Ltd is owed £10,000 by XYZ Ltd and obtains a warrant of execution on February 1st.

- DEF Ltd is owed £1,000,000 by XYZ Ltd and obtains a warrant of execution on February 2nd.

- The entire assets of XYZ Ltd are seized by the bailiff and (after all costs) the amount realised is £10,300.

- ABC Ltd gets £10,000. DEF Ltd gets £300.

The nature of the legal system

Claimants often find the legal system deeply frustrating. They know they are in the right and they think that the courts should join in and get their money for them. They do not like the technicalities. They might just understand the neutrality up to the point where judgment is obtained, but they think that not enough is done for them after that point.

A moment's pause for thought does show that neutrality up to judgment has to be correct. The whole point of a court is to decide who is right. You might know, but it has to be established. There are reasons for technicalities too. You only need to imagine yourself as a defendant. You come home from a holiday in the Himalayas to find a case has been started and finished, and that your furniture has been sold to pay a claim that you did not know existed, and which is spurious anyway. Thank goodness for technicalities.

It might be expected that a court would take a partisan approach to enforce the judgments that it makes, rather as it will enforce a penalty for contempt of court. But it will not do this. It will provide the forum for you to enforce it and it will act as a neutral umpire to see that the rules are followed. You have to pay in advance for each step that you take. It will not initiate enforcement action. Sorry! But that's the way it is.

Delays in the system may be frustrating and these are often caused by the large number of cases that have to be dealt with. Some courts are worse than others in this respect. There have been recent fundamental changes to the way that the courts operate and it is hoped that these will result in big improvements.

Delays are not just a British phenomenon. Ireland is just one country with a worse problem.

Choosing the right court

A claim may be issued in the High Court or in any county court. The choice is restricted by the monetary value of the claim and possibly by other factors. Subject to this, you may choose which to use. This is explained in detail later in Chapter 17.

Checklist

✓ Do consider enforcing retention of title; if you can and if it is sensible to do so.

✓ Do remember that the great majority of actions are uncontested. Everyone knows that the money is payable.

✓ But, if there is a genuine dispute, do try hard to resolve it.

✓ Do remember that enforcing judgment is often more difficult than obtaining judgment.

✓ If you negotiate and make concessions, do ensure that the negotiations are 'without prejudice'.

✓ Do understand that if the customer really cannot pay (as opposed to will not), there may be no point in taking legal action.

✓ Do be clear whether you are acting for commercial reasons, or as a matter of principle.

✓ Do always send a credible final warning letter, and make it a good one. This succeeds in more than 50% of all cases.

✓ Do look at your conditions of sale (if you have them and if they apply). Can they help? Can you invoice anything else? Especially, can you invoice interest?

✓ Do not be afraid of doing the work yourself, if you have time and if it is an area where it is permitted.

✓ Do consider paying a solicitor or credit agency by means of a percentage of sums actually recovered.

✓ But if you do, do not forget court costs. And consider special arrangements for a large debt with a good chance of success.

✓ If you employ a solicitor or credit agency, do stay in charge for the commercial decisions.

✓ Do resist unnecessary work. It pays to ask if it can be avoided.

✓ Do watch costs.

✓ Do get the facts right, especially the exact correct name of the defendant.

✓ Do send an example of your customer's stationery to your solicitor or credit agency.

✓ Do realise that it may pay to act quickly. Others might gain an advantage if you delay.

chapter seventeen

Legal action – obtaining judgment

Introduction

This chapter is of necessity an abbreviated summary of a large subject, though it should be very helpful. Further reading may be necessary for a person planning specific legal action. Court leaflets are often very helpful.

I do hope that you have read Chapter 16. It contains information about the courts and the legal processes, as well as practical advice on how to save money and manage your claim effectively. You will draw more benefit from this chapter, and also from Chapter 18, if you have read it.

Chapter 18 shows how to best enforce a judgment once it has been obtained, but first you have to win the case and get judgment. Winning the case is usually easy, because the great majority of actions are undefended. It is not disputed that the money is owing; it is just that the customer will not, or cannot, pay in an acceptable time.

If the action is undefended, you just have to get the technicalities right and 'victory' will be yours. Enforcing the victory and actually getting paid may present more difficulties. This chapter takes you through the technicalities, and also deals with what happens if a defence is entered.

Recent changes to the legal system

Major changes were implemented on 26th April 1999. They can be summarised as follows:

1. There is now a new unified code of procedural rules. This replaces the separate High Court rules and county court rules.

2. There is a determination to use plain English in the rules, the forms and generally throughout the system. Centuries old terms have been replaced. The following are examples of the new terms and the old terms that they replaced:

claim form	writ or summons
statement of case	pleading
claimant	plaintiff
child	minor or infant
in private	in camera
without notice	ex parte
with notice	inter partes
litigation friend	next friend or guardian ad litem
freezing injunction	Mareva injunction

3. There is now a 3 track system for dealing with cases according to the value and complexity of the case. The 3 tracks are:

   • The small claims track.

   • The fast track.

   • The multi-track.

4. Pre-action protocols set standards and timetables for the initial stages of cases before they reach court. Judges take an active role in strictly enforcing the protocols and disciplining a party that breaches them. This more active management of cases is expected to speed up throughput and increase efficiency.

Selection of route to follow

You may be able to choose one of the following four options:

- An action in the small claims court (this is the small claims track of the county court).

- An action in a county court.

- An action in the High Court.

- Winding up or bankruptcy.

Winding up relates to a company and bankruptcy relates to an individual or partnership. If the debt is at least £750, you may decide to go straight for winding up or bankruptcy, though it is unusual to do so. Winding up and bankruptcy may also be used as methods of enforcing judgment. Winding up and bankruptcy are covered in Chapter 19 and do not feature further in this chapter.

The financial limits for High Court and county court are as follows:

- The minimum claim that may be brought in the High Court is £15,000. There is no maximum figure.

- There are no minimum or maximum figures for claims that may be brought in a county court.

- The maximum figure for a claim in the small claims court is £5,000. This is the small claims track of the county court.

It follows from the above that a claim up to £15,000 must be brought in a county court. If a claim is over £15,000 the claimant may choose the High Court or a county court.

The raising of the limit to £15,000 has ensured that many more claims must be brought in a county court. To a certain extent, the unification of the procedural rules has eliminated some of the differences.

A practical reason for choosing the High Court (where this option is available), may be a wish to have enforcement carried out using the High Court. County court judgments over £600 (except those relating to a consumer credit agreement) may, at the claimant's option, be transferred to the High Court for enforcement. At the time of writing the £600 figure is subject to government confirmation.

The county court in outline

The great majority of actions are brought in the county court (including the small claims court, which is a division of it). The action may be brought, and further work done, by an individual, sole trader, partner, or company. If a person acts on behalf of a partnership or company, he must show that he is authorised to do so.

A claim in the county court may be for any amount. There are no upper and lower limits.

Procedures are generally simpler than in the High Court, and costs are generally less than in the High Court. These may be two good reasons for choosing the county court, although the differences are smaller than previously.

There are approximately 200 county courts located throughout England and Wales. They are listed in appropriate telephone directories under 'COURTS'. You may start an action in any one of them, and you might like to know that some have the reputation of being more efficient and less overworked than others.

If your action is undefended, the county court that you have chosen will deal with it throughout. If a defence is entered, the case will automatically be transferred to the county court that covers the area named as the defendant's address on the claim. This county court will conduct the hearing, if there is one, and any enforcement procedures will be in it. This could mean, for example, that an action started in a county court in Newcastle is transferred to a county court in Plymouth. This only applies when the defendant is an individual.

This transfer (if it is made) may cause delay, and it may cause inconvenience and expense. In contrast, there is only one High Court, so cases cannot be transferred. However, you may not be conveniently located for the High Court in the first place.

There are similarities to the High Court with several of the enforcement procedures. However, you should note the following differences:

- A county court warrant of execution is enforced by a county court bailiff who is a salaried person. The High Court equivalent is enforced by a Sheriff who operates on a private enterprise basis, and gets commission on what he recovers. It is widely felt that the Sheriffs achieve better results.

- Attachment Of Earnings Orders are only available through the county court, not the High Court.

- The county court may accept payment by instalments. This does not apply in the High Court, though the parties may make an informal arrangement.

The small claims court in outline

The small claims court is part of the county court. For this reason there are many similarities and much of the above applies too. It is intended that the small claims courts will be 'user friendly' and they do generally achieve this.

Formal rules of evidence do not apply and this is at the discretion of the judge. Claimants and defendants are encouraged to conduct their own case. Costs (but not court fees) are much smaller.

Claims with a limit of £5,000 may be brought in the small claims court. Due to the above advantages, claimants sometimes try to bring more than one action, each for less than £5,000. If the debt arose out of one contract, this is not permitted. You cannot claim £5,000 then come back for another £2,000 later. On the other hand, you can bring two separate cases if there are two separate contracts.

You can voluntarily limit your claim to £5,000. This might be worth considering if the amount owing is only slightly over £5,000. The amount claimed must be for full and final settlement if this is done.

Enforcement procedures are the same as for the county court. Alas, it is no easier.

The High Court in outline

There is only one High Court and it has jurisdiction throughout England and Wales. This means that a case cannot be switched, which is an advantage.

A company must use the services of a solicitor if it is bringing an action in the High Court. This does not apply to an action in the county court.

The claim must be at least £15,000. There is no upper limit. Claims below £15,000 must be made in the county court.

Procedures are generally more complex than in the county court, and costs are generally higher than in the county court.

The High Court has no facility for accepting payments in instalments, though the parties may make informal arrangements. This contrasts with the county court which does have this facility.

The High Court is reputed to take a generally tougher line about enforcing judgments. This is generally welcomed by claimants and is the most common reason for choosing the High Court.

In particular, seizure of goods is done by a High Court Sheriff. A similar function is performed by a county court bailiff. The Sheriffs are rewarded by commission. They are widely believed to be more effective than the bailiffs, who are salaried.

Steps to winning judgment

The issue of a claim

A claim form may be obtained from any county court, the High Court or from a legal stationer. The claim form should be carefully completed and this is explained later in this chapter. At least three copies of the form should be completed (one for the court, one for the claimant and one for each defendant).

The completed claim form should be taken or sent to a county court or the High Court and the appropriate fee paid. If it is in order, the claim will be issued by the court. At this stage the claim number will be allocated by the court.

Service of the claim

It is important that the claim be properly served on the defendant. If it is not properly done, the proceedings will probably be invalidated.

A county court will normally serve the claim by sending it to the defendant by post. If the defendant is an individual or partnership, the claim is deemed to be served seven days after posting. If the defendant is a company, the claim is deemed to be served two working days after posting.

Alternatively, you can ask to serve it yourself. This may be done personally, by a process server or by some other means. In this case the effective service date is the date that it is actually served. This may save time, because as well as the postal period the court may take some time to send it out.

If serving the claim is done personally, it is important that the technicalities are correctly observed. Failure to do so may invalidate the proceedings and cause extra expense.

The High Court does not post claims or arrange for service. The claimant must do it personally or arrange to have it done.

Once the claim has been validly served, strict time limits start to apply. One of these is the time given for the defendant's response.

The defendant's options on receipt of a claim

The clock starts running when the summons has been served. The defendant can respond in one of four ways.

1. Pay the amount demanded

This, of course, is the desired result and it does often happen. The defendant may pay the original sum owed, but not the validly claimed interest and costs. In these circumstances you may decide to write them off, but you are entitled to ask the court to enter judgment for them.

2. Ignore it

This quite often happens. After 14 days you may ask the court to enter judgment by default.

3. Admit the debt but not pay it

This may be done with or without a proposal for payment. The defendant is asked to send an admission form to the claimant and this form should detail the payment proposal. The claimant may accept the proposals, reject them or negotiate. If agreement is not reached, the court will eventually order a payment schedule, or perhaps order immediate payment in full. If no proposals are made, the claimant may decide what payment schedule he requires (this is not to say that the defendant will actually observe it).

4. File a defence (with or without a counterclaim)

The defence may be an assertion that the whole claim is unjustified and that nothing is payable. It may admit that part of the claim is payable, but that the remainder is unjustified. It may state that nothing is payable and that, on the contrary, money is claimed by the defendant from the claimant.

If any of these things happened, and unless subsequent agreement is reached, the matter will ultimately be resolved at arbitration or a trial.

Steps to judgment

If the defendant does not file a defence, the claimant may apply for judgment after the prescribed time has elapsed.

If the defendant does file a defence, the court will send an allocation questionnaire to each party. The information provided will be used to allocate the case to one of the three tracks.

- The small claims track (county court only).

- The fast track (county court or High Court).

- The multi track (county court or High Court).

Unless an agreement is reached, the case will progress to settlement at an arbitration or a trial. This book does not have room for a study of this.

Judgment

This will be granted (so long as the formalities are correctly observed) following:

- Victory at arbitration or a trial.

- Application following no response from the defendant.

- Application following admission by the defendant, but no payment.

The claim form in detail

The next four pages consist of the front and rear of a claim form, together with the notes for the claimant that accompany it. In order to illustrate the principles, the form has been completed to show a hypothetical claim.

The accompanying notes are very informative, but a few additional points follow the form.

Claim Form

In the	AYLESBURY
Claim No.	

Claimant

JONES AND BROWN (A FIRM)
47 HILL STREET
AYLESBURY
BUCKS
HP22 4LK

SEAL

Defendant(s)

W. FLOWERS LTD
22 BROAD STREET
LUTON
BEDFORDSHIRE
LU7 2AT
(COMPANY NUMBER 1314222)

Brief details of claim

THE CLAIM IS FOR THE PRICE OF GOODS
SOLD AND DELIVERED.
THE REMEDY SOUGHT IS PAYMENT IN FULL

Value

SPECIMEN

Defendant's name and address

W. FLOWERS LTD
22 BROAD STREET
LUTON
BEDFORDSHIRE
LU7 2AT
(COMPANY NUMBER 1314222)

	£
Amount claimed	10,200.00
Court fee	200.00
Solicitor's costs	
Total amount	10,400.00
Issue date	1ST JUNE 1999

The court office at

is open between 10 am and 4 pm Monday to Friday. When corresponding with the court, please address forms or letters to the Court Manager and quote the claim number.
N1 Claim form (CPR Part 7) (4.99)

	Claim No.	

Particulars of Claim (attached)(to follow)

THE CLAIM IS FOR £10,000 BEING THE PRICE OF AN ORIGINAL WATERCOLOUR PAINTING BY JOHN WEST ENTITLED 'RED APPLES' SOLD AND DELIVERED BY THE CLAIMANT TO THE DEFENDANT ON 1ST MARCH 1999, AND FOR INTEREST ON THAT SUM UNDER S69 COUNTY COURTS ACT 1984. THE CLAIMANT CLAIMS :

1.   £10,000.00

2. INTEREST UNDER S69 COUNTY COURTS ACT 1984 AT THE RATE OF 8% PER YEAR AMOUNTING TO £200.00 FROM 1ST MARCH 1999. THE TOTAL NOW DUE IS £10,200.00 (IE £10,000 PLUS £200.00 INTEREST)

3. INTEREST AS ABOVE FROM 1ST JUNE 1999 AT THE RATE OF £2.19 DAILY UNTIL JUDGMENT OR EARLIER PAYMENT.

SPECIMEN

Statement of Truth

*(I believe)(~~The Claimant believes~~) that the facts stated in these particulars of claim are true.
* I am duly authorised by the claimant to sign this statement

Full name   KEITH JOHN BROWN

Name of claimant's solicitor's firm _____

signed   K. J. Brown   position or office held   PARTNER

*(Claimant)(~~Litigation friend~~)(~~Claimant's solicitor~~) (if signing on behalf of firm or company)

*delete as appropriate

Claimant's or claimant's solicitor's address to which documents or payments should be sent if different from overleaf including (if appropriate) details of DX, fax or e-mail.

Notes for claimant on completing a claim form

Further information may be obtained from the court in a series of free leaflets.

- Please read all of these guidance notes before you begin completing the claim form. The notes follow the order in which information is required on the form.
- Court staff can help you fill in the claim form and give information about procedure once it has been issued. But they cannot give legal advice. If you need legal advice, for example, about the likely success of your claim or the evidence you need to prove it, you should contact a solicitor or a Citizens Advice Bureau.
- If you are filling in the claim form by hand, please use black ink and write in block capitals.
- Copy the completed claim form and the defendant's notes for guidance so that you have one copy for yourself, one copy for the court and one copy for each defendant. Send or take the forms to the court office with the appropriate fee. The court will tell you how much this is.

Notes on completing the claim form

Heading

You must fill in the heading of the form to indicate whether you want the claim to be issued in a county court or in the High Court (The High Court means either a District Registry (attached to a county court) or the Royal Courts of Justice in London). There are restrictions on claims which may be issued in the High Court (see 'Value' overleaf).

Use whichever of the following is appropriate:

'In the ....County Court'
(inserting the name of the court)

or

'In the High Court of Justice........................Division'
(inserting eg. 'Queen's Bench' or 'Chancery' as appropriate)
'.............................District Registry'
(inserting the name of the District Registry)

or

'In the High Court of Justice........................Division,
(inserting eg. 'Queen's Bench' or 'Chancery' as appropriate)
Royal Courts of Justice'

Claimant and defendant details

As the person issuing the claim, you are called the 'claimant'; the person you are suing is called the 'defendant'. Claimants who are under 18 years old (unless otherwise permitted by the court) and patients within the meaning of the Mental Health Act 1983, must have a litigation friend to issue and conduct court proceedings on their behalf. Court staff will tell you more about what you need to do if this applies to you.

You must provide the following information about yourself **and** the defendant according to the capacity in which you are suing and in which the defendant is being sued. When suing or being sued as:-

an individual:

All known forenames and surname, whether Mr, Mrs, Miss, Ms or Other (e.g. Dr) and residential address (**including** postcode and telephone number) in England and Wales. Where the defendant is a proprietor of a business, a partner in a firm or an individual sued in the name of a club or other unincorporated association, the address for service should be the usual or last known place of residence **or** principal place of business of the company, firm or club or other unincorporated association.

Where the individual is:

under 18 write '(a child by Mr Joe Bloggs his litigation friend)' after the name. If the child is conducting proceedings on their own behalf write '(a child)' after the child's name.

a patient within the meaning of the Mental Health Act 1983 write '(by Mr Joe Bloggs his litigation friend)' after the patient's name.

trading under another name

you must add the words 'trading as' and the trading name e.g. 'Mr John Smith trading as Smith's Groceries'.

suing or being sued in a representative capacity

you must say what that capacity is e.g. 'Mr Joe Bloggs as the representative of Mrs Sharon Bloggs (deceased)'.

suing or being sued in the name of a club or other unincorporated association

add the words 'suing/sued on behalf of' followed by the name of the club or other unincorporated association.

a firm

enter the name of the firm followed by the words 'a firm' e.g. 'Bandbox - a firm' and an address for service which is either a partner's residential address or the principal or last known place of business.

a corporation (other than a company)

enter the full name of the corporation and the address which is either its principal office **or** any other place where the corporation carries on activities and which has a real connection with the claim.

a company registered in England and Wales

enter the name of the company and an address which is either the company's registered office **or** any place of business that has a real, or the most, connection with the claim e.g. the shop where the goods were bought.

an overseas company (defined by s744 of the Companies Act 1985)

enter the name of the company and either the address registered under s691 of the Act **or** the address of the place of business having a real, or the most, connection with the claim.

N1A Notes for claimant (4.99)

Brief details of claim

Note: The facts and full details about your claim and whether or not you are claiming interest, should be set out in the 'particulars of claim' *(see note under 'Particulars of Claim').*

You must set out under **this** heading:

- a concise statement of the nature of your claim
- the remedy you are seeking e.g. payment of money; an order for return of goods or their value; an order to prevent a person doing an act; damages for personal injuries.

Value

If you are claiming a **fixed amount of money** (a 'specified amount') write the amount in the box at the bottom right-hand corner of the claim form against 'amount claimed'.

If you are not claiming a fixed amount of money (an 'unspecified amount') under 'Value' write "I expect to recover" followed by whichever of the following applies to your claim:

- "not more than £5,000" **or**
- "more than £5,000 but not more than £15,000"**or**
- "more than £15,000"

If you are **not able** to put a value on your claim, write "I cannot say how much I expect to recover".

Personal injuries

If your claim is for 'not more than £5,000' and includes a claim for personal injuries, you must also write "My claim includes a claim for personal injuries and the amount I expect to recover as damages for pain, suffering and loss of amenity is" followed by either:

- "not more than £1,000" **or**
- "more than £1,000"

Housing disrepair

If your claim is for 'not more than £5,000' and includes a claim for housing disrepair relating to residential premises, you must also write "My claim includes a claim against my landlord for housing disrepair relating to residential premises. The cost of the repairs or other work is estimated to be" followed by either:

- "not more than £1,000" **or**
- "more than £1,000"

If within this claim, you are making a claim for other damages, you must also write:

"I expect to recover as damages" followed by either:

- "not more than £1,000" **or**
- "more than £1,000"

Issuing in the High Court

You may only issue in the High Court if one of the following statements applies to your claim:-

"By law, my claim must be issued in the High Court. The Act which provides this is ....(specify Act)"

or

"I expect to recover more than £15,000"

or

"My claim includes a claim for personal injuries and the value of the claim is £50,000 or more"

or

"My claim needs to be in a specialist High Court list, namely..................................(state which list)".

If one of the statements does apply and you wish to, or must by law, issue your claim in the High Court, write the words "I wish my claim to issue in the High Court because" followed by the relevant statement e.g. "I wish my claim to issue in the High Court because my claim includes a claim for personal injuries and the value of my claim is £50,000 or more."

Defendant's name and address

Enter in this box the full names and address of the defendant receiving the claim form (ie. one claim form for each defendant). If the defendant is to be served outside England and Wales, you may need to obtain the court's permission.

Particulars of claim

You may include your particulars of claim on the claim form in the space provided or in a separate document which you should head 'Particulars of Claim'. It should include the names of the parties, the court, the claim number and your address for service and also contain a statement of truth. You should keep a copy for yourself, provide one for the court and one for each defendant. Separate particulars of claim can either be served

- with the claim form **or**
- within 14 days after the date on which the claim form was served.

If your particulars of claim are served separately from the claim form, they must be served with the forms on which the defendant may reply to your claim.

Your particulars of claim must include

- a concise statement of the facts on which you rely
- a statement (if applicable) to the effect that you are seeking aggravated damages or exemplary damages
- details of any interest which you are claiming
- any other matters required for your type of claim as set out in the relevant practice direction

Address for documents

Insert in this box the address at which you wish to receive documents and/or payments, if different from the address you have already given under the heading 'Claimant'. The address must be in England or Wales. If you are willing to accept service by DX, fax or e-mail, add details.

Statement of truth

This must be signed by you, by your solicitor or your litigation friend, as appropriate.

Where the claimant is a registered company or a corporation the claim must be signed by either the director, treasurer, secretary, chief executive, manager or other officer of the company or (in the case of a corporation) the mayor, chairman, president or town clerk.

It is better to put too much detail rather than too little, provided of course that the detail is correct.

If the defendant is a sole trader using a trading name, a title should be used such as 'Peter Higgins Trading as Cut Price Bananas'.

If the defendant is a partnership, the correct name of the partnership should be used followed by 'A Firm'.

If the defendant is a company, the exact correct name of the company should be quoted. It is good practice to quote the registered office address and the company registration number. The registered office address must, by law, be registered at Companies House. Proof of service to the registered office is proof of good service. A company cannot 'go away' from its registered office. It must notify Companies House of the address of a new registered office. Although it is good practice to name the registered office, it is not essential. A significant company address can be used instead.

'Brief details of claim' calls for a very few sentences that sum up what the claim is all about. The specimen form uses 'the price of goods sold and delivered' which is an extensively used phrase.

Full details of the claim are given on the second page. A separate sheet may be used for this if necessary. The specimen form sets out a hypothetical claim in detail and you might like to look at this closely. It shows how to calculate and claim interest at the statutory rate. At the time of writing this is 8%.

Footnote – summary judgment

It is, regrettably, fairly common for defendants to seek time by filing an extremely weak or bogus defence. They may do this with no serious expectation of winning a case, or even do so with no intention of actually presenting the case in court. It is just a device to gain time and possibly cause the claimant to give up in frustration. There is a procedure to overcome this, and it is available in both the county court and the High Court.

The claimant swears a short affidavit, stating the facts and stating his belief that there is no defence to the claim. A copy is sent to the defendant who has a chance to respond. An early hearing will be held and if the court is satisfied that the money is owing, judgment will be entered. If the court believes that the defendant has an arguable case, the application for summary judgment will be rejected and the case will progress to a full trial.

The summary judgment procedure is open to abuse, and claimants should only use it when they have good reasons for believing that there is not a valid, arguable defence. It should be noted that a weak defence is not the same thing as no defence. The court is likely to be displeased if the process is abused.

Checklist

✓   Do treat this chapter as a helpful introduction, not as a comprehensive guide.

✓   Do read Chapter 16 as well as this one.

✓   Do remember that the technicalities are important. Failure to observe them can frustrate an action, even if it is a strong case.

✓   Do particularly remember that the status of the defendant must be correctly quoted, and that the name and address should be exactly right.

✓   Do select the best legal route with care.

✓   Do remember that cases, in the county court and small claims court, may be transferred to the defendant's local court. This will happen if a defence is entered, or if enforcement procedures are taken.

✓   Do consider that the High Court is generally thought to take a tougher line on enforcement.

✓   Do remember that High Court Sheriffs are generally thought to be more effective than county court bailiffs.

✓   Do remember that the small claims court is 'user friendly'. There is minimum formality and low costs.

✓   Do remember that the small claims court can only be used for claims up to £5,000.

✓   Do remember that serving a claim must be done properly. Otherwise, it may not count.

✓   Do remember that the option of the small claims court is now more available and attractive than ever before.

✓   Do remember that you can claim interest as well as the principal sum.

✓   Do consider applying for summary judgment if the defendant enters a bogus defence. But remember that the court will be displeased if you misuse the application.

chapter eighteen

Legal action –
enforcing the judgment

Introduction

Enforcing judgment, and actually getting paid, is frequently more difficult than obtaining the judgment in the first place. If the defendant ignores the whole thing it is easy to get judgment, provided that you observe the technicalities. But if the defendant continues to ignore the whole thing after judgment, you have to force something to happen. Inertia does not work to your advantage.

It will be extremely difficult if the customer has very little money, and impossible if he has no money at all. It may be difficult if the customer actively tries to frustrate you, or, to a lesser extent, adopts a 'don't care' attitude.

Enforcing judgment is not a fail-safe system. Nothing will happen unless it is made to happen. Court fees are payable in advance, and they are payable whether recovery is successful or not. They are recoverable from the debtor, but of course they must be actually obtained, along with the original debt. A further difficulty is that the court may order payment by installments, and you may feel that this forces you to wait too long, even if the installments are regularly paid.

Most of the different enforcement procedures may only be used one at a time, not simultaneously. You cannot, for example, obtain an attachment of earnings order against a judgment debtor, then seize his assets as well. It has to be one or the other, and you have to abandon one in order to start the other one.

There are often practical benefits to be obtained in acting quickly and decisively. If there are other judgments you will be in competition, and you may lose if you delay. Many enforcement proceeds are applied in the order in which the orders are granted, not pro rata, and not in the order in which judgment was obtained. Consider the following example:

- A Ltd obtains judgment against X Ltd for £2,000 on September 4th.

- B Ltd obtains judgment against X Ltd for £2,000 on September 8th.

- B Ltd obtains a warrant of execution on October 12th.

- A Ltd obtains a warrant of execution on October 14th.

- The bailiff seizes assets belonging to X Ltd and sells them (after expenses) for £400. B Ltd gets £400 and A Ltd gets nothing.

All this may be slightly depressing, although realistic. Now let us look on the bright side. You are in the right, you have obtained judgment, the law is there to be used and numerous people do use it very successfully. The remainder of this chapter studies how to enforce judgment and get paid.

The rest of the chapter is allocated separately to the county court and the High Court. The small claims court is part of the county court and enforcement procedures are the same.

Enforcing judgment

Enforcing judgment in the county court (including the small claims court)

If the customer fails to pay a judgment debt, or fails to keep up with instalments ordered by the court (even by one day), you may apply for enforcement proceedings.

County court money judgments up to £600 must be enforced in the county court. County court money judgments over £600 may, at the option of the claimant, be transferred to the High Court for enforcement by a Sheriff. At the time of writing this limit of £600 is subject to government confirmation. However, judgment for debts regulated by a consumer credit agreement must be enforced in the county court, regardless of the amount of the judgment.

If enforcement is in the county court, it must be in the court that covers the judgment debtor's address. This can be a disadvantage, and it really does mean that a case can be transferred from Carlisle to Southampton.

The following methods of enforcement are available in the county court, and this chapter considers them each in detail:

- Warrant of execution.

- Garnishee order.

- Attachment of earnings order.

- Charging order.

- Appointment of a receiver.

- Bankruptcy or winding up.

Warrant of execution

This is an order for the county court bailiff to seize the debtor's goods, and sell enough of them to pay the total outstanding amount of the judgment debt, plus interest to date. The costs of the execution must also be paid, and this has first call on any money raised. Warrant of execution is by far the most commonly used enforcement method.

The county court bailiff will not act as a detective in tracking down assets. He will only visit addresses supplied to him, and it is extremely helpful to supply known details of assets that might be taken. Jointly owned assets may be taken, but the bailiff may not take:

- Assets owned by a partner (common law wife or husband).

- Assets owned by a landlord or any other person.

- Assets subject to a hire purchase agreement.

- Assets that the debtor reasonably needs to conduct his business, such as the tools of his trade.

- Essential household items, such as bedding.

- Debtor's personal clothes.

The above exclusions can present a lot of practical problems, and this may be exploited by an unscrupulous debtor. It can be very difficult to establish the precise ownership of assets.

The bailiff will endeavour to either remove goods immediately, or by entering into a 'walking possession' agreement. This involves identifying specific goods, but leaving them in the debtor's possession. If a walking possession agreement applies, it is an offence for the debtor to remove or dispose of the particular goods. If payment is not made within a specified period, the bailiff returns and removes the goods.

Goods seized by the bailiff are sold at public auction without a reserve. The proceeds go first to pay the bailiff's costs and then to the creditor. Any amount left over is returned to the debtor.

Amounts raised at the auctions are often disappointing, and such auctions often provide spectacular bargains for observant buyers. Items such as second-hand furniture and second-hand electrical goods may not be taken, because they are bulky and often realise very small amounts.

The arrival of a county court bailiff may be a terrible shock to some debtors. It is the moment when they are forced to face reality. Quite a number manage to find the money at this point, or very soon afterwards. Or they come up with a serious proposal for paying by installments.

The debtor may pay a fee and ask for the warrant to be suspended (stopped). If he does this he must make proposals for paying the debt and give the court (and the creditor) details of his financial affairs. The creditor may accept the debtor's proposal, but if he rejects them the court will rule on the matter.

On the following page there is an example of a completed request for a warrant of execution.

Request for Warrant of Execution

to be completed and signed by the plaintiff or his solicitor and sent to the court with the appropriate fee

1 Plaintiff's name and address

JONES AND BROWN (A FIRM)
47 HILL STREET
AYLESBURY
BUCKS
HP22 4LK

In the

AYLESBURY **County Court**

Case Number 45 31313

2 Name and address for service and payment (if different from above) **Ref/Tel No.**

0129-611 111

3 Defendant's name and address

MRS MAVIS SMITH
18 JUNIPER ROAD
AYLESBURY
BUCKS
HP22 7

SPECIMEN

4 Warrant details

(A) Balance due at date of this request	600	00
(B) Amount for which warrant to issue	600	00
Issue fee	40	00
Solicitor's costs		
Land Registry fee		
TOTAL	640	00

If the amount of the warrant at (B) is less than the balance at (A), the sum due after the warrant is paid will be

I certify that the whole or part of any instalments due under the judgment or order have not been paid and the balance now due is as shown

Signed L. Brown (PARTNER)

Plaintiff (Plaintiff's solicitor)

Dated AUGUST 18ᵗʰ 1988

IMPORTANT
You must inform the court immediately of any payments you receive after you have sent this request to the court

---

Other information that might assist the bailiff including the name(s) and address(es) of any 2nd/3rd defendant and other address(es) at which the defendant might have goods. You should also tell the court if you have reason to believe that the bailiff might encounter serious difficulties in attempting to execute the warrant.

MRS SMITH OWNS A BLUE BMW 525 CAR REGISTRATION NUMBER H136 SRO. IT IS KEPT IN THE GARAGE AT THE REAR OF HER HOUSE.

Warrant No.

Garnishee order

This is an order by the court to someone who owes money to the judgment debtor. It orders this third party to freeze the debt (hold the money) until directed by the court as to who should be paid.

'Someone who owes money' encompasses 'some body that owes money'. Garnishee orders are commonly directed to banks and building societies. A bank account in credit does represent money owing by the bank to the account holder.

Garnishee orders can be attached to most debts owing to the judgment debtor. This includes trade debts owing to a business. So if General Electric Company PLC owes money for supplies this may be garnisheed. It also includes wages owing, rent owing, private loans, and many other types of debts.

Garnishee orders may not be attached to maintenance orders, legacies and one or two other things. You should note the following restrictions and features:

- Only money actually due on the date issued may be garnisheed. If the debtor earns £3,000 per month and is paid at the end of each month, you cannot get £1,500 by garnisheeing the employer on the 15th of the month. Similarly rents can only be garnisheed when they are contractually due. If a debt is due, but not yet payable, such as a debt on 60 day payment terms, it may be garnisheed.

- Banks and building societies must only pay money actually in the account when the garnishee order is issued. If the garnishee order is for £10,000, the bank account is £300 in credit, and £12,000 is credited to the account the next day, only £300 may be paid over by the bank.

- The debtor does not know until afterwards that a garnishee order has been issued. So you have the advantage of surprise. Otherwise, the debtor could remove the money before the order takes effect.

It may pay to use the element of surprise to maximum effect. First of all you should try to obtain as many details about the debt as possible. If it is a bank account, it is best to have the branch, account name and account number.

It may also be a good idea to time your action for maximum effect. If you know that a significant sum is coming into the account, you should time your action to take effect immediately after receipt and before the money is paid out. Salaries are commonly paid towards the end of a month, and commonly go out of the account by standing orders, etc, at the beginning of the following month. It may pay to time your action at the very end of a month.

The following is an outline of the procedure:

- You make an application for a garnishee order. This is done on the special form. You must swear an affidavit concerning the debt. Needless to say, an oath should not be sworn irresponsibly.

- The court will consider the application. It may issue a garnishee order and fix a date for the hearing.

- The order need not be served on the judgment debtor for a period of seven days. During this period the garnishee order may take effect.

- A hearing will be held if necessary. The judgment debtor may attend and dispute the facts. The court will consider all the circumstances, including the behaviour and needs of the judgment debtor, and including the interests of other people who may have claims.

- Following the hearing, the court will order how the frozen money is to be allocated and paid.

Attachment of earnings order

An attachment of earnings order is an order to an employer to withhold money from the judgment debtor's wage or salary. The use of these orders has considerably increased in recent years. They were used extensively to collect the Community Charge (Poll Tax) and are now used for the Council Tax. They are widely used by the Child Support Agency and are open to others to use in the same way.

By definition, an attachment of earnings order may only be used against an individual in employment. It may not be used against limited companies, partnerships, the self-employed, or the unemployed.

An attachment of earnings order may apply to wages and salaries, overtime, bonuses, commission, etc. It may also apply to pensions paid by an employer. It does not apply to state pensions, and it does not apply to social security benefits.

The court will consider the debtor's financial circumstances and his reasonable commitments and needs. It may then make an order for an employer to deduct a fixed amount per week or month. It will fix a level of protected earnings. This is an amount (after deductions for tax and national insurance contributions) which the employee is allowed to keep before deductions are made. If a deduction cannot be made one week or month, it is permanently lost. It is not made up in succeeding deductions. This can best be illustrated with an example:

An order is for deductions of £10 per week and the level of protected earnings is fixed at £400 per week.

- *In week 1 earnings are £460 and £10 is deducted.*

- *In week 2 earnings are £402 and £2 is deducted.*

- *In week 3 earnings are £399 and nothing is deducted.*

- *In week 4 earnings are £500 and £10 is deducted.*

Attachment of earnings orders are widely used. They tend to be most effective when the debtor is in stable employment, earns reasonable money and has modest commitments. This, of course, is exactly the sort of person least likely to owe money in the first place. Attachment of earnings orders suffer from the following disadvantages:

- A separate order must be taken out every time the debtor changes his employer. This can be troublesome and expensive.

- The debtor may not earn enough to make it worthwhile.

- An unscrupulous debtor may frustrate the order by frequently changing jobs, becoming self-employed, becoming unemployed, or by deliberately earning less than the protected amount. An even more unscrupulous debtor may take undeclared earnings from the black economy.

A creditor may obtain an attachment of earnings order by filling in the appropriate form and paying the appropriate fee. The judgment debtor is required to provide full details of his assets, liabilities, income and obligations. The court will then fix a hearing which the judgment debtor may be required to attend.

Charging order

A charging order gives the applicant a registered legal interest in property, or stocks and shares, owned by the judgment debtor. This puts him in the same secured position as (for example) a bank that has registered a charge as security for an overdraft. The charging order will rank behind any charges that already exist.

The court has the power to order the asset to be sold but it frequently will not exercise that power. It may think that it is out of proportion for a house (for example) to be sold in order to pay off a relatively small debt. However, it may sometimes order the asset to be sold, particularly if the debt is large and the asset can quickly, easily and cheaply be sold. Some financial securities come within this definition. If the asset is ordered to be sold, the person taking out the charging order should get paid relatively quickly.

Often, the court will not order the asset to be sold, leaving the charge in existence. This means that the applicant will get the money when the asset is sold, perhaps many years later. It also means that no future charges may be created on that asset that rank ahead of the charging order.

Appointment of a receiver

This is not used very often and is at the court's discretion.

The court (after an application supported by an affidavit) may appoint a receiver to exercise powers normally exercised by the judgment debtor. An example of the receiver's use of his power would be to collect rents that become payable over a period of time in the future. A garnishee order, by contrast, can only freeze rents owing at the time that it is issued.

Bankruptcy or winding up

Bankruptcy applies to an individual. Winding up applies to a limited company. Application may be made if the unsatisfied judgment debt is at least £750.

There is considerable expense and potential disadvantages, but the threat may be very effective in forcing the judgment debtor to do his best. Of course, bankruptcy and winding up do sometimes take place, and are sometimes justified.

The subject is covered in detail in the next chapter.

These are the county court remedies available if a judgment debtor does not pay. Before moving on to the High Court, there are two other county court matters that should be examined; oral examination and the registration of county court judgments.

Oral examination

A procedure exists to force the debtor to disclose details of his assets and liabilities, income and commitments. As in other sections of this chapter the word 'he' is used for all judgment debtors, including women, partnerships and limited companies.

Knowledge may enable you to act in the most effective way to ensure payment. For example, the debtor may own few assets but hold a highly paid job. In these circumstances you would probably get details of the employer, then apply for an attachment of earnings order. There would be little point in applying for a warrant of execution.

The debtor may be instructed to appear before the court for an oral examination. If he fails to appear he will be instructed again, and if he fails to appear again (without a good reason), he may be committed to prison. A partner may be examined about the affairs of a partnership, and a director may be examined about the affairs of a limited company.

The court may ask the questions or the creditor may request permission to ask reasonable questions himself. The debtor should have been instructed to bring with him such things as payslips and bank statements.

It sounds frightening and the powers of the court sound enormous, as indeed they are. However, they are not always used in the firm way that many creditors would wish. Relatively few debtors are committed to prison, either for not turning up or for not co-operating. Excuses and requests for extra time to get details are sometimes accepted.

The main advantage can be its deterrent value. It can be a frightening prospect and it may give a debtor an incentive to act reasonably. However, it may sometimes elicit useful information.

Oral examination is a way of getting information. It is not an enforcement method. Enforcement may be conducted afterwards or separately.

The register of county court judgments

All unpaid county court judgments are registered. This is done at:

Registry Trust Ltd
173/175 Cleveland Street
London W1P 5PE

Telephone: 0207 380 0133

The judgment debtor may apply to have the entry removed from the register if one of the following applies:

- The full amount of the judgment debt has been paid within one month and proof of this can be supplied.

- The judgment has (at any time) been 'set aside' by the court. A court may set aside the judgment either because it is wrong, or so that the claim can be defended.

If a judgment debt remains unpaid for a month, it will, unless it is set aside, remain on the register for six years. This is so, even if it is subsequently paid in full.

An entry on the register of county court judgments is a serious impediment to getting future credit, and it is a serious handicap for a business. It is therefore an incentive for the debtor to pay the judgment debt within a month.

The register may be searched to discover if there have been any judgments recorded against a specific person (or business) at a specific address. A fee is payable for each search. The information is one indication as to whether it is worth bringing an action or trying to enforce a judgment. If there are a large number of recent judgments, all for large amounts, there is probably not much point.

The High Court

County court money judgments for more than £600 may, at the option of the claimant, be transferred to the High Court for enforcement. The figure of £600 is subject to government confirmation and judgments relating to consumer credit agreements (regardless of the amount) must be enforced in a county court. Of course, most High Court judgments are enforced in the High Court, but in some cases a transfer to a county court may be made.

The High Court is generally more formal than the county court, and it is generally believed to take a tougher line on the enforcement of judgments.

High Court enforcement procedures are very similar to county court enforcement procedures, and for this reason they are only examined in outline. The High Court has the facility for oral examinations in a similar way to the county court. The following are the High Court enforcement procedures:

Writ of Fieri Facias

This corresponds to a warrant of execution in the county court. It appoints a High Court Sheriff to seize the goods of the judgment debtor.

Charging order

Garnishee order

Appointment of a receiver

Attachment of earnings orders do not exist in the High Court. Enforcement in the county court is necessary for one to be issued.

Checklist

✓ Do remember that enforcing judgment may be much more difficult than obtaining judgment.

✓ Do realise that nothing will happen, unless you make it happen and pay for it in advance.

✓ Do accept that the rewards often go to those who are quick and decisive. Other creditors may get in first.

✓ Do give the county court bailiff (and the High Court sheriff) all the helpful information that you can. It often makes a big difference.

✓ Do realise that county court bailiffs are often deluged with cases. Also realise that sums realised at auction (after expenses) may be disappointing.

✓ If you use a garnishee order, do use surprise and good information, and time it well.

✓ If the debtor is an individual in stable employment, do consider an attachment of earnings order. But it may take a long time to clear the debt.

✓ Do remember that a charging order may be suitable when there is an asset such as property. But you might have to wait (whilst earning interest) for years.

✓ Do remember that impact on the debtor is very important. The threat of bankruptcy or winding up may have the most impact of all.

✓ Do think if the debtor knows about the Register of county court judgments, and that only payment within a month will get his name removed. If you think that he does not know; tell him.

✓ Do remember that High Court sheriffs are generally considered to be more effective than county court bailiffs.

chapter nineteen

Winding up, bankruptcy, administration orders and receivers

Introduction

Many areas are covered by the title to this chapter. Administration orders and receivers are studied in the latter part, but winding up and bankruptcy are taken first. They have quite a lot in common, and may be a final step in the enforcement of judgment. Alternatively, they may take place independently of what has been described in Chapter 17 and Chapter 18.

You probably knew it already, and you know it if you have read the previous chapters. Nevertheless, to make sure, the following is the difference between winding up and bankruptcy.

- Winding up applies to a company.

- Bankruptcy applies to an individual or a partnership. Insolvent sole traders may be made personally bankrupt.

The threat of winding up and bankruptcy

If a company can pay a debt, and does not wish to be wound up, the credible threat of winding up proceedings almost invariably produces payment. This applies to companies big and small, but especially big. Similarly, a credible threat of personal bankruptcy often succeeds, so long as the debtor has some money, does not wish to be made bankrupt, and is capable of bringing a minimum amount of discipline to his probably chaotic affairs. On balance, the threat of bankruptcy is probably slightly less effective than the threat of winding up.

Actually winding up a company, or making a person bankrupt, is not an attractive option in many cases, especially if the debt is small and there is a big deficiency. There are significant costs and you do not get priority over other creditors. However, it may be even less attractive to the company or person threatened.

All threats should be credible, but it is worth pointing out that the threat costs virtually nothing. A statutory demand may be obtained from a firm of law stationers. It is a frightening and official-looking form, and will probably upset the person opening the envelope. It is likely to annoy as well as upset the recipient. You almost certainly do not wish to take further orders from the debtor, but sending a statutory demand will probably reduce the chances to absolute zero.

The courts rather disapprove of winding up and bankruptcy proceedings being used as a routine credit control procedure. Nevertheless, it is their duty to uphold the law and they will apply it. Fred Williams the window cleaner really can take steps to wind up a major public company, so long as the debt is at least £750, the facts support him, and he follows the technicalities. Of course the major public company does not actually get wound up. It pays Fred the money, which is the object of the exercise.

If you get past the statutory demand stage you should be very careful to only claim what is clearly and unambiguously owing. Do not on any account claim any items subject to a reasonable dispute. You will annoy the court, and annoy your solicitor if you have one, and may have to pay some unwelcome costs.

Procedures

Winding up procedures

Winding up or bankruptcy proceedings may be brought against a judgment debtor. But obtaining judgment is not a necessity. The threat, and then the reality, can be applied straight away. It does very often work.

Winding up orders can only be given in respect of companies registered in this country. They cannot be given for companies registered abroad.

Winding up is very often a voluntary process instigated by the company itself, and this may happen whether the company is solvent or insolvent. However, these notes concern just winding up instigated by a creditor. The steps in the process are as follows:

- A correctly completed statutory demand form must be sent to the registered office of the company. The debt must be at least £750.

- The company has 21 days to make the payment.

- After 21 days a petition may be presented to the High Court (or some county courts). This must be in the required form and give the required details. The applicant must file an affidavit in support of the petition.

- The court will seal the petition which is served on the company.

- The petition is advertised in the *Gazette*.

- The petition is heard by the court which may reject it, adjourn it, or issue a winding up order.

- If a winding up order is issued, the company must provide a statement of its affairs to the official receiver, who becomes the provisional liquidator. The directors are relieved of their powers and the assets of the company are vested in the official receiver.

- A liquidator is appointed, and he realises the assets for the benefit of the creditors, in accordance with the statutory rules.

- Ultimately, the company is struck off the register and ceases to exist.

It is important to note that the creditor that presented the petition does not get priority in the ultimate distribution. He ranks equally with the other creditors.

Bankruptcy procedures

Bankruptcy procedures are similar to winding up procedures, and for this reason are not set out here. Of course, at the end of the day, the bankrupt does not cease to exist in the same way that a struck-off company ceases to exist. A very sad (in most cases) person is left to pick up the pieces of his life. Some bankrupts are wicked, many are irresponsible, but some are just very unlucky. The bankrupt Lloyds of London 'names' are an example of the latter. Illness and uninsured catastrophe are two factors that can lead to disaster. For these reasons creditors sometimes do not press bankruptcy procedures, even if the situation warrants it.

There is more than one statutory demand form to individuals which can be issued as a prelude to a possible bankruptcy petition. The following two pages are the Statutory Demand for use when an individual has not satisfied a judgment debt. It is a four page document, but the other two pages are almost blank pages for details to be inserted.

Statutory Demand
under section 268(1)(a)
of the Insolvency
Act 1986.
Debt for Liquidated
Sum Payable
Immediately
Following a Judgment
or Order of the Court
(Rule 6.7)

NOTES FOR CREDITOR
- If the Creditor is entitled to the debt by way of assignment, details of the original Creditor and any intermediary assignees should be given in part C on page 3.
- If the amount of debt includes interest not previously notified to the Debtor as included in the Debtor's liability, details should be given, including the grounds upon which interest is charged. The amount of interest must be shown separately.
- Any other charge accruing due from time to time may be claimed. The amount or rate of the charge must be identified and the grounds on which it is claimed must be stated.
- In either case the amount claimed must be limited to that which has accrued due at the date of the Demand.
- If the Creditor holds any security the amount of debt should be the sum the Creditor is prepared to regard as unsecured for the purposes of this Demand. Brief details of the total debt should be included and the nature of the security and the value put upon it by the Creditor, as at the date of the Demand, must be specified.
- Details of the judgment or order should be inserted, including details of the Division of the Court or District Registry and Court reference, where judgment is obtained in the High Court.
- If signatory of the Demand is a solicitor or other agent of the Creditor, the name of his/her firm should be given.

* Delete if signed by the Creditor himself.

WARNING

- This is an **important** document. You should refer to the notes entitled "How to comply with a Statutory Demand or have it set aside".
- If you wish to have this Demand set aside you must make application to do so **within 18 days** from its service on you.
- If you do not apply to set aside **within 18 days** or otherwise deal with this Demand as set out in the notes **within 21 days** after its service on you, you could be made bankrupt and your property and goods taken away from you.
- Please read the Demand and notes carefully. If you are in any doubt about your position you should seek advice **immediately** from a solicitor or your nearest Citizens Advice Bureau.

DEMAND

To

Address

SPECIMEN

This Demand is served on you by the Creditor:

Name

Address

The Creditor claims that you owe the sum of £
full particulars of which are set out on page 2, and that it is payable immediately and, to the extent of the sum demanded, is unsecured.

By a Judgment /Order of the High Court   /

County Court in proceedings entitled

(Case) Number   between

                                                           Plaintiff
and   Defendant
it was adjudged/ordered that you pay to the Creditor the sum of £
and £   for costs.

The Creditor demands that you pay the above debt or secure or compound for it to the Creditor's satisfaction.

[The Creditor making this Demand is a Minister of the Crown or a Government Department, and it is intended to present a Bankruptcy Petition in the High Court in London.] [Delete if inappropriate].

Signature of individual

Name
(BLOCK LETTERS)

Date   day of   19

*Position with or relationship to Creditor:
*I am authorised to make this Demand on the Creditor's behalf.

Address

Tel. No.   Ref. No.

N.B. The person making this Demand must complete the whole of pages 1, 2 and parts A, B and C (as applicable) on page 3.

[P.T.O.

1

Part A

Appropriate Court for Setting Aside Demand

Rule 6.4(2) of the Insolvency Rules 1986 states that the appropriate Court is the Court to which you would have to present your own Bankruptcy Petition in accordance with Rule 6.40(1) and 6.40(2).

Any application by you to set aside this Demand should be made to that Court, or, if this Demand is issued by a Minister of the Crown or a Government Department, you must apply to the High Court to set aside if it is intended to present a Bankruptcy Petition against you in the High Court (see page 1).

In accordance with those rules on present information the appropriate Court is [the High Court of Justice] [County Court]
(address)

Part B

The individual or individuals to whom any communication regarding this Demand may be addressed is/are:
Name ....
(BLOCK LETTERS)

Address ....

....

Telephone Number ....

Reference ....

Part C

For completion if the Creditor is entitled to the debt by way of assignment.

	Name	Date(s) of Assignment
Original Creditor		
Assignees		

How to comply with a Statutory Demand or have it set aside (ACT WITHIN 18 DAYS)

If you wish to avoid a Bankruptcy Petition being presented against you, you must pay the debt shown on page 1, particulars of which are set out on page 2 of this notice, within the period of **21 days** after its service upon you. However, if the Demand follows (includes) a Judgment or Order of a County Court, any payment must be made to that County Court (quoting the Case No.). Alternatively, you can attempt to come to a settlement with the Creditor. To do this you should:
- inform the individual (or one of the individuals) named in Part B above immediately that you are willing and able to offer security for the debt to the Creditor's satisfaction; *or*
- inform the individual (or one of the individuals) named in Part B above immediately that you are willing and able to compound for the debt to the Creditor's satisfaction.

If you dispute the Demand in whole or in part you should:
- contact the individual (or one of the individuals) named in Part B immediately.

If you consider that you have grounds to have this Demand set aside or if you do not quickly receive a satisfactory written reply from the individual named in Part B whom you have contacted you should **apply within 18 days** from the date of service of this Demand on you to the appropriate Court shown in Part A above to have the Demand set aside.

Any application to set aside the Demand (Form 6.4 in Schedule 4 of the Insolvency Rules 1986) should be made within 18 days from the date of service upon you and be supported by an Affidavit (Form 6.5 in Schedule 4 to those Rules) stating the grounds on which the Demand should be set aside. The forms may be obtained from the appropriate Court when you attend to make the application.

> **Remember:** From the date of service on you of this document:
> (a) you have only **18 days** to apply to the Court to have the Demand set aside, and
> (b) you have only **21 days** before the Creditor may present a Bankruptcy Petition.

3

Wrongful trading

Directors may be guilty of wrongful trading if they carry on trading when they know, or ought to know, that there is no reasonable prospect of avoiding insolvent liquidation. The courts have the task of interpreting the word 'reasonable' and it can be a matter of fine judgment.

Wrongful trading may apply to all directors, including non-executive directors. This can sometimes come as a nasty shock to those not actively involved in running the company. The liquidator must, in the case of an insolvent liquidation, make a report to the Department of Trade and Industry. It is usual for him to write to all creditors to ask if there is anything concerning directors' conduct that should be drawn to his attention.

If a court decides that a director has been guilty of wrongful trading, it may disqualify him from being a director for between two and fifteen years. In fact these powers are used very sparingly, and the level of proof required is high. The courts are sometimes criticised for not taking a tougher line, and there are regular scandals concerning directors who have been involved with many failed companies.

If wrongful trading is proved, you may be able to set aside limited liability and make directors personally liable for debts. This is a separate matter to disqualification, and one does not necessarily follow from the other. Again, the burden of proof is high and it does not happen very often.

Administration and receivership

The remainder of this chapter deals with administration and receivership. This is not liquidation, though it does often lead on to liquidation later.

For many years, up to 1986, the law relating to companies in difficulties had generally been considered inadequate. Too many companies foundered that might have been saved. The law dated from a bygone age, and there were far too many scandals concerning company directors and also liquidators.

All this led to the Insolvency Act 1986 which is now the principal act regulating administration and receivership. The aims of the act included:

- A very big reduction in the number of scandals and abuses.

- To be as fair as possible to all parties.

- To save companies that could be turned round.

After more than a decade, it is probably fair to say that there have been big improvements, but that the aims have not entirely been achieved. It is certainly true that there are now fewer scandals and abuses. But the number of companies saved has been rather disappointing. One common complaint has been that holders of security (especially banks) have acted in a ruthless way to recover their loans and protect their own interests. There are now some signs that things are improving, and that more savable companies are actually being saved.

Administration orders and receivership are considered separately, then licensed insolvency practitioners, and finally there is practical advice for creditors confronted with administration or receivership.

Administration orders

The object of an administration order is to:

- Save the whole company (or failing that, part of the company) so that it escapes its problems and continues to trade.

or failing that

- To enable a favourable realisation of the company's assets to take place.

An application for an administration order may be made by the directors of the company, or by one or more creditors, or by some combination of directors and creditors. During the period between the presentation of the petition and its hearing by the court, the following restrictions apply:

- No liquidation proceedings may be commenced.

- No debt recovery or enforcement proceedings may be commenced. Any existing such proceedings are frozen.

- No security can be enforced.

- Repossession of goods held under hire purchase or leasing agreements is not allowed.

- Retention of title may not be enforced.

The court may, if appropriate, give its permission for all but the first of the above restrictions to be lifted.

If the court makes an administration order the administrator must call a meeting of creditors within three months to consider his proposals. The creditors meeting may approve the proposals, reject them, or (with the consent of the administrator) amend them.

Whilst an administration order is in force there is a general moratorium. All the above restrictions continue to apply and, in particular, you should note that retention of title may not be enforced. However, the administrator may not dispose of such assets without the court's permission.

Administration is subject to the court's supervision, and it comes to an end when the court so directs, usually at the request of the administrator, but occasionally at the request of the creditors.

Receivership

An administrative receiver is appointed by a debenture holder. This is usually, but not always, a bank. Receivership may be general, or the receiver may act only concerning certain specified assets.

The receiver's main job is to see that the assets and business are best protected. This is for the benefit of the debenture holders and then for the other creditors afterwards.

The receiver must report to the general creditors within three months of his appointment. Ordinary creditors may continue to exercise retention of title rights.

Licenced insolvency practitioners

Prior to 1986 almost anyone could be a liquidator or receiver, and some rather strange people did hold these positions. Of course in most cases they were responsible, especially if appointed to large companies, but there were abuses. The press dubbed one character 'Hissing Sid', and his like were regularly exposed by Esther Rantzen and others.

Now it is different. Insolvency practitioners have to be licensed. They must hold one of the approved professional qualifications and they must uphold certain standards. This has led to some complaints that they can be unduly expensive, but they are professional.

They can (like all of us) make mistakes, and they can (with or without good reason) infuriate creditors. They can seem slow and bureaucratic. They have a difficult job and, after all, they are appointed because a company has got itself into a mess. Some conflict is almost inevitable.

Practical advice

You will rightly be concerned to hear that a receiver or administrator has been appointed. It frequently comes as a nasty surprise to creditors. They may be about to lose some or all of their money, and their power to act is extremely limited.

You must receive the reports within the specified time scale and this should give you better information. In the case of an administration order you can use your vote. However, if you are a small creditor it probably will not make too much difference. In practice, it is nearly always sensible to support the administrator's proposals.

If you have retention of title, and it is a receivership, you may decide whether or not to exercise it.

In many cases the major decision is whether or not to make further supplies if asked to do so. Whatever the powers of administrators and receivers they only relate to past contracts. They do not have the power to make you enter into a future contract. A licensed insolvency practitioner is very unlikely to request a future delivery for which you will not be paid, so you can draw a lot of comfort from this. On the other hand you may have to wait rather a long time for the money.

Your decision may be influenced by the attitude towards outstanding debts, and your power will depend on how badly your supplies are needed. If you supply sausage rolls for the Christmas party then your power is very limited, especially if the date is January 6th. On the other hand an electricity company probably has total power to shut down a company. Utilities, such as electricity suppliers, are sometimes criticised for exercising their power ruthlessly.

Checklist

✓ Do remember that a credible threat to make a person bankrupt, or especially to wind up a company, may be very persuasive.

✓ Do remember that if a company has the means to pay, and does not wish to be wound up, it is almost guaranteed to pay. But the threat must be credible, and payment may be at the last minute.

✓ Do, of course, remember that such a threat will probably kill any chance of future business.

✓ Do not present a petition unless you are sure of your facts and there is not a reasonable dispute.

✓ Do not claim more than is definitely owing. It may be expensive if you do.

✓ Do consider acting with other creditors. It spreads the costs.

✓ Do be careful to get the technicalities right.

✓ Do remember that in winding up and bankruptcy, the creditor that presents (and pays for) the petition, does not get priority.

✓ Do think about wrongful trading, but not for too long. In practice it is rarely made to stick.

✓ Do consider exercising retention of title if you are able to do so. You are not normally permitted to do this if there has been an application for an administration order.

✓ Do consider confronting a receiver or administrator with any muscle that you have. Of course, you might not have any.

chapter twenty

Bad debts

Introduction

It would be nice to think that this chapter is being read only as a matter of academic interest. Unfortunately this would not be very realistic. Any business with more than just a few credit customers is likely to have at least an occasional bad debt.

Bad debts are inevitable for a business that makes significant sales on credit, particularly if made directly to the public. Managers of such a company should budget a certain percentage of sales as a bad debt reserve. Having done this they should take strenuous steps to keep the number of bad debts as small as realistically possible, and to minimise their losses. A company giving credit to just a few customers may avoid bad debts, at least for a time. When one does occur it can be a nasty shock, especially if it is unexpected or the amount is large.

As a matter of practical management it is usually necessary to balance a wish to boost sales with a wish to keep bad debts to a minimum. Exactly how this is done and where the balance is struck is a matter for judgment in individual cases.

The common understanding of a bad debt is that it is what happens when a customer goes bust. Common understanding is wrong. A better definition of a bad debt is that it happens when either:

> a customer cannot pay
>
> OR
>
> a customer will not pay and you are unable or unwilling to take the necessary steps to force him to pay.

Furthermore the amount of the bad debt may be reduced by any VAT that can be reclaimed, by any stock that may be recovered, by any dividend that may be paid by the debtor, and by any amount covered by credit insurance.

Having made that clear the rest of this chapter deals with what happens when a customer 'goes bust'. The following are the steps that you can take to protect your position and minimise the loss.

How to minimise the loss

Get back the VAT

Prior to 1990 the debtor had to be declared formally insolvent (winding up or bankruptcy) before VAT bad debt relief could be obtained. The rules were significantly eased in 1990 and, in summary, VAT bad debt relief can now be obtained when the following applies:

- Six months have elapsed from the latest of the invoice date, the date of supply of goods or services, and the contractual date for payment.

- VAT on the original supply has been accounted for.

- The debt has been written off in the supplier's books.

- The original goods were to be paid for in cash at a commercial value on an arm's-length basis.

- Title to goods must have passed to the buyer (this applies to supplies made from 19th March 1997).

These are the circumstances in which VAT bad debt relief may be claimed. There are two obligations of which you should be aware:

- Within seven days of your claim for VAT bad debt relief you must, if your customer is VAT registered, give him details.

- Your claim for VAT bad debt relief must be made within three and a half years of the latest of the invoice date, supply of goods or services, and the contractual date for payment.

In practice you do not always know whether or not your customer is VAT registered, so it is sound policy to notify customers in all cases. This may have the (for you) beneficial effect of stirring the customer into action. Of course if the customer is insolvent, or cannot pay, it will not do so, but if he can he may take fright.

The customer will realise that he has to hand back VAT that he has claimed which will affect his cash flow. He will also think that he has been drawn to the attention of H.M. Customs and Excise and that unpleasant consequences may follow. He must repay the VAT that he has deducted and it may increase the likelihood of a VAT inspection.

In fact many customers will be ignorant about the fine detail of VAT law and Customs and Excise procedures. They will look at your letter and think just one thing, 'TROUBLE'. With luck it may be even worse, they could panic. This is excellent news for you. At an absolute minimum it draws it to the customer's attention and he may well be worried. It is a good idea to word your letter to increase this sense of alarm. The following is an example of a letter that might achieve this, whilst at the same time fulfilling your legal obligations.

Example of a good letter notifying a customer of a claim for VAT bad debt relief

The Company Secretary
Bladon Software Ltd
18 Croft Street
Witney
Oxfordshire

December 19 1998

Dear Sir

Notification of Report to Customs and Excise

As required by law, I am writing to notify you that you have been reported to Customs and Excise. This company has claimed VAT bad debt relief of £1,750.00 in respect of our valid invoice number 12354 to you for £11,750.00 dated December 22 1997.

If you have claimed a deduction of £1,750.00 on this invoice, you may be required by law to repay it. Customs and Excise may require to inspect all records relating to this transaction, may check to see that repayment of the VAT has been made, and may conduct a general inspection of your VAT records.

This company has not abandoned its claim to payment of £11,750.00. It is our intention to vigorously pursue payment and instigate legal proceedings.

Yours faithfully

P Patel
Credit Controller

The obligation to write off the debt in your books is an oblig-ation to do so in internal management accounts, if prepared. Of course, write off in the signed statutory accounts must follow later. There is no need to wait for the signed statu-tory accounts before making the claim.

There is an obvious practical advantage in having specific bad debt reserves in the accounts, rather than a general bad debt reserve of x per cent. Only in this way can you claim the VAT bad debt relief; a general reserve will not do. The same applies for income tax relief (for a sole trader or partnership) or corporation tax relief. Your accountant will presumably have told you this, but if not show him or her this Guide.

Customs and Excise requires you to keep precise records. If payment (in full or in part) is received after VAT bad debt relief has been claimed, payment of the VAT (in full or in part) must be made to Customs and Excise. This must be done in the next VAT return after payment has been received.

All the above is illustrated by the following example.

It is assumed that ABC Ltd makes a delivery on February 1st, raises an invoice for £10,000 plus £1,750 VAT on February 6th, and that payment is on 60 day terms (due April 6th).

It is further assumed that ABC Ltd makes up its VAT returns quarterly to March 31st, June 30th, September 30th and December 31st. ABC Ltd decides on May 19th that it will probably be a bad debt. On the following February 20th the customer pays 50% of the debt.

What happens is as follows:

Year 1

- ABC Ltd raises an invoice for £11,750 on February 6th.

- ABC Ltd accounts for £1,750 VAT in its VAT return for the quarter to March 31st.

- ABC Ltd decides on May 19th that it will be a probable bad debt. It creates a specific bad debt reserve in subsequent management and statutory accounts.

- ABC Ltd claims VAT bad debt relief of £1,750 in its VAT return for the quarter to December 31st (usually due by January 31st in Year2).

- ABC Ltd notifies its customer that it has claimed VAT bad debt relief of £1,750, and does so within seven days of making the claim.

Year 2

- Customer pays £5,875 on February 20th.

- ABC Ltd adjusts the specific bad debt reserve accordingly.

- ABC Ltd accounts for £875 VAT in its VAT return for the quarter to March 31st.

Look hard at the conditions of sale

Conditions of sale were studied in detail in Chapter 15. When you face a potential bad debt it is a good time to look hard at the conditions of sale to see if they can help you. More likely than not, they will not be able to help you. This is because many suppliers do not have conditions of sale, and many of those that do, fail to take steps to ensure that they govern the contract. But if you do have conditions of sale, and if they do govern the contract, then do have a close look.

In a business relationship it is quite normal for a supplier not to invoice every last penny that a strict interpretation of the contract would enable him to bill. This may be because it is waived in the interests of a long-term relationship. When you have a bad debt there is not going to be a long-term relationship. You should get the short-term benefits by billing everything that you can. The possibilities will vary from case to case, but the following are among the things to consider:

- Are there any penalty clauses that could be invoked?

- Is it contractually possible to charge for ancillary items such as travel or training?

- Is it possible to raise late invoices for old business as well as invoices for current items?

- Does the contract entitle you to charge interest on outstanding invoices and perhaps previous late payments?

The last point is an important one and it may be worth referring back to Chapter 15. Note particularly that you may be able to charge interest on late payments over several years, not just on the present balance.

The Late Payment of Commercial Debts (Interest) Act 1998 enables victims of late payment to charge statutory interest, and this takes effect in stages. Full details are given in Appendix A. A claim for interest under the terms of this Act should be seriously considered.

A customer's insolvency or liquidation may lead to a payment of x pence in the pound. Quite often there is not enough to fully satisfy the secured creditors and the preferential creditors. When this happens the payment to ordinary creditors will be nil pence in the pound, and increasing the amount of the debt will not achieve anything.

On the other hand, it will increase the return if there is some dividend. For example consider a debt of £20,000 where there is a dividend of 50p in the pound. The dividend would be £10,000 and the bad debt £10,000. Now let us assume that ancillary invoicing increases the debt to £22,000 and as a result the dividend drops to 49p in the pound. The dividend would be £10,780, an improvement of £780.

Liquidators, bankrupts and other suppliers sometimes claim that what I am suggesting is not ethical. It sometimes results in a deficiency (on bankruptcy or winding up) being significantly higher than had been expected. It is possible to see their point of view, but suppliers facing a bad debt have rights too. It is up to you to make up your own mind.

The situation is usually a competitive one and any gain that you make will be at the expense of other creditors. It is rare for an individual trader or company owner to personally suffer. This is because the total assets amount to a given sum and you are taking a greater share. If the customer is a limited company the owners will not suffer beyond losing their investment in it.

Even if company owners have given personal guarantees to a bank they will not usually lose. This is because banks are normally preferential creditors and their repayment ranks before ordinary creditors. In the case of a bankruptcy the bankrupt's deficiency becomes larger, but you cannot have less than nothing. It is true that sole traders or partners will suffer personally if they have to (and are able to) contribute to a deficiency.

Needless to say, I am only advocating the invoicing of what is legitimately and contractually due. Anything beyond this would be dishonest and should not be considered.

Consider enforcing retention of title

This was explained fully in the chapter on conditions of sale. The following is an outline of the conditions that must exist in order for a retention of title clause to be effective:

- Your terms must apply.

- You must be able to relate specific stock to specific unpaid invoices.

- You must give credit in full (including VAT) for stock taken back.

- You can only repossess by agreement or by invoking the law. You do not have the right of forcible removal.

- You cannot take goods that have been mixed with other goods or altered. For example you can only take leather that you have supplied, not shoes made from that leather.

- You can only repossess from your customer, not from someone who has bought from your customer in good faith.

Careful thought should be given before an attempt is made to enforce a retention of title clause. You have the job of satisfying the liquidator that your claim is a sound one and you have the administrative job of identifying your stock. You have the job of loading the stock, transporting it, and putting it back into your warehouse. All this will be at your expense.

You must give full value for what you take even though it might not still be worth as much. The stock may have lost value if it is soiled or if it is a fashion item.

You would in any case have got back the VAT on the recovered stock, and the apparent saving will not be quite so large for this reason.

I am not saying that you should not repossess stock if entitled to do so. Usually you should. I am saying that all points should be considered and that the benefits may not be quite so large as hoped for. Also, of course, you can only repossess what is still there.

Liquidators and receivers are in practice likely to be sceptical about retention of title claims. They will make you show that the terms match the circumstances, and they will make you show that your terms governed the contract. Just exhibiting your terms on an invoice or unsigned order is unlikely to be enough. They will have access to legal advice and make you prove your claim. This is fair enough and if you think that your claim is a good one you should be prepared to do so.

You should let the liquidator or receiver know that you have a retention of title claim as soon as you hear that one has been appointed. You are likely to be sent a form seeking information about the claim, asking for a copy of the terms, and seeking proof that they apply to the contract. Some of the information sought is likely to be relevant, some irrelevant, and some bordering on the impertinent. This is partly because it will be a standard form designed to cover all eventualities, and partly because the liquidator or receiver wants to protect his legal position. It is also because you are not his customer and he has no incentive to make it easy for you.

The liquidator or receiver is likely to specify a time when you can visit the premises and identify stock that is the subject of your retention of title claim. The time and date specified may be inconvenient and some time in the future. This will be done without admitting that your retention of title claim is valid. When he (or his legal adviser) has ruled on the validity of the claim you will be given an appointment when the stock (if the claim is accepted) may be removed.

Liquidators and receivers are professionally qualified people with a difficult job. They may be deluged with people making claims and demanding priority, particularly in the early days after the appointment. They deserve help and sympathy. But they do not deserve to be able to prejudice your rights and hinder your pursuit of a legitimate claim. The following is step by step practical advice on how to make and enforce your claim:

- Satisfy yourself that your claim is valid. If it is not, the remainder of the steps do not apply.

- Telephone the liquidator or receiver and notify him of your claim.

- Confirm the existence of your claim in writing. Warn that your stock must not be moved, damaged or inter-mingled. Ask for an early appointment to inspect and identify your stock.

- Fill in the inevitable form promptly. Be sporting, and even fill in some of the irrelevant parts.

- Do not accept an unreasonable delay. Warn the liquidator or receiver that you will hold them respon-sible for any harm to your rights. If necessary get your solicitor to write a letter.

- Attend the premises to identify your stock. Mark it and ensure that it is secure. If it is not, complain in writing and give details.

- Remind, pursue, nag and generally harass the liquidator or receiver. Needless to say this should only be done if he deserves it.

- Obtain confirmation that your terms apply. Get an appointment to remove the stock. Keep precise records and issue a full accurate credit note.

This sounds harsh and it is often not necessary. But sometimes it is.

You can take it from me that liquidators and receivers do respond to pressure (if you have a good case). Like the rest of us they like an easy life and they do not like trouble. They positively hate the thought of legal action. This may be bluff because you probably do not want this either, even if your case is very good. You would only want to do it as a matter of principle, or if your claim is a significant one.

Personal liability

If a person is trading in his own name, without forming a limited company, he will be personally liable for the debts. The same applies to partnerships where the individual partners will have what is known as joint and several liability. This means that the personal assets of all partners are available to pay the debts of the partnership.

The ultimate cost of personal liability is bankruptcy and either alone, or with other creditors, you may take steps to make the debtor bankrupt. In practice this is often not done, particularly if the debtor's conduct has not been too bad and if the deficit is not too large. Human feelings sometimes prevent the steps being taken, but one must also consider the costs of bankruptcy and the realistic prospects of dividends from the bankrupt.

The owners of a limited liability company do not normally have personal liability for the debts. However, in practice they often give personal guarantees to banks or other lenders. It is open to a supplier to demand personal guarantees in support of supplies to a limited company. It is not often done, and is likely to be strongly resisted. Nevertheless, it is an option which should sometimes be considered.

It sometimes happens that an individual trades as a company whilst leading suppliers to believe that he is trading with personal liability. For example, his note paper and other stationery may not disclose the existence of a company as is required by law. In these circumstances you may well succeed in holding the trader personally liable for the company debts.

Directors may be disqualified from acting as a director for a specified number of years, and may be personally liable for company debts, if their conduct falls below a certain standard. In particular, this may happen if they carry on trading when they know, or ought to know, that there is no reasonable prospect of avoiding insolvent liquidation.

Licensed insolvency practitioners have an obligation to make a report on the conduct of directors. With this in mind they often ask creditors if there are any matters which they wish to bring to their attention. In practice it is rare for a director to be made personally liable for the debts of a limited company, and a high standard of proof is required.

The legal process of liquidation

If the liquidation is expected to be an insolvent one, the proceedings will be under the control of the creditors. The initial meeting of creditors will choose and appoint the liquidator who will make reports to the creditors during the course of the liquidation. A committee of creditors will monitor the liquidation throughout its progress. Voting at the creditors' meeting, including voting on the appointment of the liquidator, is according to the amount of creditors' claims. So the milkman and the newsagent cannot get together and outvote a major supplier.

The notice convening the meeting of creditors gives each creditor an opportunity to attend and vote. The notice will be accompanied by a form of proxy which you may use if you wish. In order to cast a vote at the meeting you must send in the form certifying that you are a creditor.

You may decide to ignore the whole business which is what many creditors do. For many small suppliers this may be a sensible attitude. The costs of involvement may well exceed the benefits, and a small supplier may not have much influence anyway. You must, though, supply proof of debt on the appropriate form. If you do not do this you will not participate in any dividend that may ultimately be paid.

You may decide to attend the meeting of creditors and cast your vote personally. Alternatively you may decide to use the proxy form and have someone represent you. It is not a good idea to sign the form in blank and return it. This is because your vote will then be cast by the chairman of the meeting who will probably be a director of the failed company. Now that liquidators have to be licensed insolvency practitioners there are fewer abuses. Nevertheless, you will probably want to resist the idea of the directors choosing the liquidator.

You may be able to get most of the advantages of attending without actually doing so. This can be done by appointing a professional to represent you. Accountants, lawyers, and various credit specialists are often pleased to do this, and they usually do it without charging a fee.

Your representative will give you an independent report afterwards, and he will cast your vote. This may be in accordance with your instructions, or he may exercise his own judgment. This service is of course provided because the professionals want to see and be seen, and hope to attract work to their firms. They are usually keen to do this even if it is a small debt.

And finally – learn the lessons

A bad debt represents the ultimate failure. Do not brood too much because an occasional bad debt is inevitable for most who supply on credit. Nevertheless, you should monitor both the number of bad debts and the amounts lost. Neither should be higher than an acceptable percentage, given all the circumstances. When a bad debt occurs you should ask some searching questions.

- Was it bad luck or bad judgment?

- Was the amount of the debt bigger than it should have been?

- Would any reasonable steps have avoided the bad debt?

- Are there any lessons to be learned?

There are two things that you should *not* do:

- Do not spend too much time and energy on bad debts. Of course be sensible, but do not be obsessed and waste time.

- Do not waste too much time apportioning blame, especially if it is you yourself who is at fault.

Checklist

✓ Do console yourself. Some bad debts are virtually inevitable if you supply a significant number of accounts on credit.

✓ Nevertheless, do take reasonable steps to avoid bad debts.

✓ If applicable, do always get back the VAT as soon as possible.

✓ Do look hard at your conditions of sale, if you have them, and if they govern the contract.

✓ Do consider everything that can legitimately be invoiced.

✓ Do invoice interest (on back items too) if permitted to do so.

✓ Do consider everything legal and within the terms, but do not go beyond that.

✓ If applicable, do consider enforcing a retention of title clause, but realise that results maybe disappointing, and it is not always the best thing to do.

✓ Do take a vigorous line when presenting a legitimate retention of title claim to a liquidator or receiver.

✓ Do consider if personal liability might apply. You probably do not want to pursue it, but you just might.

✓ Do consider asking a professional to represent you at a creditors' meeting.

✓ Even if you ignore liquidation proceedings,
do establish your claim. Then you will
participate in any dividend.

✓ Do spend a little time learning the lessons,
but not too much.

chapter twenty-one

Exports

Introduction

Ensuring prompt and complete payment for export sales may have all the problems of getting prompt and complete payment for UK sales, plus some extra ones as well. Differences in language, laws and customs can cause extra complications. It is difficult to generalise and circumstances vary from country to country.

If you are accomplished in collecting UK debts, you will be part way towards being effective at collecting export debts. Most of the chapters in this Guide are partially or wholly relevant. Export credit control is a very big subject and it is not possible to completely cover the subject in one chapter. However, the following is an introduction to some of the main considerations.

The law governing the sale

It does not automatically follow that the contract is governed by the laws of England (or Scotland). It may be, but it will not necessarily be the case. For this reason it is a good idea to make it clear in the conditions of sale.

Of course, the buyer may want the contract governed by the laws of his own country. If so, you have a problem and a point for negotiation. This of course assumes that you want the contract governed by the laws of England. You probably do, if only because these will be the most familiar to you.

It is quite possible, by mutual agreement, to have the contract governed by the laws of a third country. Two contracting foreigners sometimes elect to have their contracts governed by the laws of England. Similarly, the U.S. state of Maryland is a popular choice.

If the contract is governed by the laws of one of the countries comprising the UK, statutory interest will apply. This is as provided for by the late Payment of Commercial Debts (Interest) Act 1998. This may be an advantage.

Agreement of conditions of sale

This is important when the buyer and seller are both British, but it is even more important when exports are involved. You may have to convince a foreign buyer, and perhaps a foreign court, that your conditions apply. So you must make it absolutely clear and, best of all, get a signature on the order or contract.

Some of the main conditions of sale

These will vary according to the different markets and other factors. The following are some of the main points that should be considered:

Method of payment

This is considered in detail later in this chapter. It is very important that the method of payment is agreed in advance.

Currency and currency risk

Most exporters want the contract denominated in sterling. However, it may be a good selling point to have it denominated in the buyer's currency. The currency of a third country can be nominated; the U.S. Dollar and the German D. Mark being commonly chosen. It should be very clear where the exchange risk lies; usually it is with the buyer which is where you want it. But do not forget that in this context the word 'risk' can mean a gain as well as a loss.

Retention of title

This is examined in depth elsewhere in this Guide. It is, in principle, equally valid for export sales, though there may be extra difficulties in enforcing it. The concept is widely known in some countries, Germany being a good example, but not in others.

Period of credit

This is always important, no less for exports than for UK sales. It should be absolutely clear when payment is due and when payment becomes overdue. With some methods of payment, the period of credit is geared to some form of collection within your control. In some cases the onus is on the customer to pay on the due date.

Interest on late payment

This is valid exactly as for a UK sale. In some countries the practice is more widely accepted.

Responsibility for insurance

This is particularly important in the case of exported goods. The last thing that you want is an uninsured loss. It is normally the exporter's responsibility up to delivery.

All the conditions of sale that are important for a UK sale are also important for an export sale. You will need to take it on a case by case basis.

Methods of payment

The following are the most common methods, listed in order from the most secure to the most insecure:

Payment in advance

Congratulations! No further comment is necessary.

Documentary letter of credit

This provides security for both parties. It is agreed in advance that payment will be made when certain conditions are satisfied and certain valid documents presented.

The method is for the customer to request his bank to issue the letter of credit, listing the document and timetable acceptable. Provided that these are presented in order, payment is made.

The documents and conditions can vary considerably but may include invoices, bill of lading, insurance certificate, certificate of origin, etc.

Letters of credit may be irrevocable or revocable. Obviously, irrevocable letters of credit are more beneficial for the exporter. Provided that the conditions are exactly fulfilled payment is virtually certain.

In practice, the conditions of documentary letters of credit are not exactly met in more than 50% of cases. This happens for example, when the documents presented are not exactly as specified. This does not mean that payment is not made and in nearly all cases it ultimately is. But it does mean that the exporter's security is lost.

Bill of exchange

The exporter prepares a bill of exchange and sends it to the customer. If it is a sight bill it is payable immediately. A term bill is payable either on a specified date or a specified number of days after sight or after a certain event such as shipment. The person to whom the bill is addressed is required to accept it by signing the face. An accepted bill is required to be paid on the due date and may be discounted in advance of that date.

Open account

There is no security at all in this method and in that it is similar to most UK sales. The conditions of sale will normally state that payment is due a certain number of days after delivery. The purchaser is then required to remit the money on the due date.

Documentation

The importance of correct documentation

Some of the payment methods work with release of payment on production of specified documents. There are variations, and variations in the documents required. The buyer's security is that he does not lose control of the money until the goods are at a certain point within his control. The exporter's security is the opposite; he does not lose control of the goods until payment is ensured.

The requirements are very often (and for understandable reasons) interpreted by banks and others in a pedantic way. The documents have to be exactly as specified. Nearly, as specified will not do. You are therefore required to get things exactly right. This is a matter of skill, training and an eye for detail.

If the documents are not exactly right the exporter may well lose his security. If the problem is just a technicality he will be relying on the buyer to authorise payment anyway, and will have the right to take other action if necessary.

Some of the main documents explained

Commercial invoice

This normally shows considerable detail and is often produced in sets. The customer may need more than one, and other parties (insurer, bank, etc) may need them. Commercial invoices will show full details of the goods shipped, weights, dimensions, number of cartons, etc. It will show the basis of payment (CIF, FOB, etc) and details of the payment term and how payment is required.

Consular invoice

Some countries require an invoice to be stamped and authorised by their embassy or consulate in the exporter's country. This is so that they can allocate foreign exchange, keep accurate records, etc. It is a significant chore for the exporter and may be a disincentive to export to those countries, which may be the unacknowledged reason why it is required. The contents of a consular invoice are the same as those of a commercial invoice.

Pro forma invoice

This is an invoice prepared ahead of shipment. It may be required by the buyer and should be the same as the eventual commercial invoice.

Certified invoice

Some countries insist that invoices be certified by a Chamber of Commerce or similar body.

Certificate of origin

Some countries require certification of where the goods origi- nated. In some cases certification by some body such as a Chamber of Commerce is required. In other cases certifi- cation by the exporter is sufficient.

Bill of lading

This is issued by the shipper, usually signed and in sets of three. It is the title to the goods, which must be presented by the consignee. It also serves as a receipt, to the exporter, that the shipper has taken possession. A clean bill of lading indicates that the goods were accepted complete and undam- aged. A clean bill of lading is usually required to facilitate release of the goods and payment. Similar documents are issued by airlines.

Insurance certificate

It is normal for significant exporters to have an overall policy to cover (within limits) all shipments that they make. Insur- ance certificates are issued for each shipment against this overall policy.

Bill of exchange

This is prepared by the exporter and sent to the customer, sometimes directly and sometimes via a bank. The customer is asked to pay it immediately (in the case of a sight draft), or to accept it (in the case of a term draft). A term draft may be discounted (subject to the standing of the drawee) and is payable after a stated number of days or after a stated event (e.g. shipment).

Frequently used abbreviations and their definitions

FOB	Free on board
FAS	Free alongside ship
C and F	Cost and freight
CFR	Cost and freight
CIF	Cost, insurance and freight
EXQ	Ex. quay
EXS	Ex. ship
EXW	Ex. works
DDP	Delivered duty paid

The importance of good information

Good information is always important, but especially so in the case of export customers. Local agents and local distributors may be a good source.

Credit agencies may come into their own. Some credit agencies offer only a UK service, but others may have good foreign information. Some are part of an international group and some have links to agents in other countries. Others specialise in certain markets and territories. If in doubt, it is a good idea to start with one of the big agencies with a well known name. Intrum Justita and Dun and Bradstreet are two examples.

Factoring and credit insurance

This Guide contains separate chapters on each of these two subjects. Both services are widely available to exporters and may be well worth considering. They include:

- Payment up front (in the case of factoring)

- Credit insurance

- Information

- Informal advice and assistance

- Help with collection (in the case of factoring)

Checklist

✓ Do remember that conditions of sale are especially important.

✓ Do make sure that the contract or order is legally enforceable, and preferably signed.

✓ Do make sure that English law governs the contract, if this is what you want.

✓ Do have method and time of payment clearly specified in the contract.

✓ Do be clear who bears the currency risk. Do remember that there may be risk of a gain as well as risk of a loss.

✓ Do be clear whose responsibility it is to insure and at what point the insurance cover terminates.

✓ Do get the technicalities of the export documentation exactly right. This may be a burden but it is important. You may well forfeit your protection if you make a mistake.

✓ Do remember that good information is particularly important.

✓ Do consider factoring and credit insurance. Both may be very helpful.

appendix A

Legislation relating to statutory interest on late payment of debt

Legislation relating to statutory interest on late payment of debt

This appendix is a summary of the provisions of the Late Payment of Commercial Debts (Interest) Act 1998.

Debts to which the act applies

The Act applies to commercial debts only. This means a debt where both debtor and creditor are acting in a business capacity. It does not apply, for example, to a consumer credit agreement, a hire purchase debt or a mortgage.

Size of debt

There are no upper or lower limits to the size of the debt.

The rate of interest

This is 8% over bank base rate. It is simple interest, not compound interest. A contract, or custom and practice may take precedence, but only if they provide a 'substantial remedy'.

Stages in which the act takes effect

The Act takes effect in three stages:

- Contracts made from 1st November 1998 – small businesses against large enterprises and the public sector.

- Contracts made from 1st November 2000 – small businesses against all enterprises and the public sector.

- Contracts made from 1st November 2002 – all businesses and the public sector against all enterprises and the public sector.

Definition of a small business

A small business is one that employed, on average, less than 50 during the previous financial year. Part time staff are counted pro-rata.

The period that must elapse before statutory interest will apply

Where a payment period is specified in a contract, that payment period will generally apply. However, it will only apply if the contract provides a 'substantial remedy'.

Where no period is agreed, or where the contract does not provide a substantial remedy, payment will be due on the later of:

a) 30 days from delivery or performance of the service.

b) 30 days from the customer being notified that payment is required. This nearly always means by the sending of an invoice.

Possibility of contracting out

It is not possible to contract out of statutory interest, even if both parties wish to do so. However, the victim of late payment may choose not to enforce his rights.

A contract normally takes precedence over the Act, provided that it provides a 'substantial remedy' for late payment. If it does not do so, the Act will override the contract.

Custom and practice may set the terms. However, this can only be the case if it provides a 'substantial remedy' for late payment. If it does not do so, custom and practice will be overridden by the Act.

Disputes

Invoices that are genuinely and reasonably disputed are excluded.

appendix B

Companies House addresses and details

Companies House addresses and details

For companies registered in England and Wales

Crown Way
Maindy
Cardiff CF4 3UZ
Tel 01222 388 588

21 Bloomsbury Street
London WC1B 3QW
Tel 01222 388 588

Satellite offices

75 Mosley Street
Manchester M2 2HR
Tel 01222 388 588

Birmingham Central Library
Chamberlain Square
Birmingham B3 3HQ
Tel 01222 388 588

25 Queen Street
Leeds LS1 2TW
Tel 01222 388 588

For companies registered in Scotland

37 Castle Terrace
Edinburgh EH1 2EB
Tel 0131 535 5800

Satellite office

21 Bothwell Street
Glasgow G2 6NL
Tel 0141 248 3315

Availability from each office

Records of companies registered in England and Wales are normally available in a maximum of two hours at the Cardiff and London offices. They are available within 24 hours at the Manchester, Birmingham and Leeds offices.

Records of companies registered in Scotland are normally available in a maximum of two hours at the Edinburgh office and within 24 hours at the Glasgow office.

Records of Scottish companies are available within 24 hours at the English and Welsh offices. Records of companies registered in England and Wales are available within 24 hours at the Scottish offices. Records of companies registered in Northern Ireland are available at 48 hours notice in all offices.

Method of identification

Every company has a unique registration number and this number must be quoted to obtain the information. It is a legal requirement that the registration number be quoted on company stationery. The correct number may be obtained from an alphabetical index, but there are over a million companies on it.

Outline of information available

Records for each company are normally kept on three microfiches as follows:

Fiche A: Annual accounts and annual returns and information updating these records.

Fiche M: Details of any mortgages or charges (not all companies have a Fiche M).

Fiche G: All other documents.

These normally go back three years. Information for up to about another 22 years is available on further (weeded) fiches.

Methods of application

A.   By personal application to any of the offices

B.   By postal application

This should be to either the Cardiff or Edinburgh offices. A fiche or paper copy is normally mailed the same day. Order may be by a simple telephone call or by post. Unless an account has been opened, pre-payment must be made by cheque or credit card.

C.   On-line application

This facility is now available. The necessary equipment is required.

Examples of some of the main charges

Search room services

Standard search (microfiche)	£5.00
Requests for information not on fiche (hard file)	£6.00
Inter-registry search	£5.00
Screen prints	10p
Fiche copies of bulk shareholders list (any number of sheets)	£5.00
Weeded accounts microfiche (per company)	£5.00

Postal and fax services

Microfiche copy of a company record ordered by post or telephone	£8.00
Microfiche copy of weeded accounts ordered by post or telephone	£8.00
Paper copy of company documents ordered by post or telephone	£9.00
Further document relating to the same company requested on the same occasion	£2.50
Registered office address by telephone	No charge
Fax search (per document)	£12.00

Directors register company – based enquiry:

- by fax   £5.00
- by post   £4.00

appendix C

Court fees payable in connection with legal action to recover debt

Court fees payable in connection with legal action to recover debt

The following fees are correct at the time of publication. They are adjusted periodically, usually in an upward direction. There are other fees but these are the ones most likely to be encountered.

The county court

(this includes the small claims court)

To issue a claim

To issue a claim where the claim is for money only and the amount of the claim is not more than:

£200	£20
£300	£30
£400	£40
£500	£50
£1,000	£70
£5,000	£100
£15,000	£200
£50,000	£300
Over £50,000	£400

If you are making a counterclaim, you must pay a fee corresponding to the above. For example, if your counterclaim is for £550 you must pay a fee of £70.

General fees

On the filing of an allocation questionnaire by
the claimant   £80

On the claimant filing a listing questionnaire or
where the court fixes the trial date or trial week
without the need for a listing questionnaire:

   a) if the case is on the multi-track   £300

   b) in any other case (this does not apply to   £200
       a small claims hearing)

On filing notice of an appeal   £100

On an application by consent or without notice
for judgment or order where no other fee is
specified   £25

On an application to vary a judgment or suspend
enforcement   £25

Taxation (assessment of costs)

On the filing of a request for detailed assessment:

   a) where the party filing is legally aided   £80

   b) where the party filing is not legally aided   £120

On an application for the issue of a default costs
certificate   £40

On an appeal against a decision made in detailed
assessment proceedings   £50

Enforcing judgments

Warrants (bailiff)

To issue a warrant of execution to recover a sum of money:

a) where the sum of money to be recovered is not more than £125   £25

b) where the sum to be recovered is more than £125   £45

On a request for a further attempt at execution of a warrant at a new address   £20

Garnishee order

To issue an application   £50

Receiver

To issue an application   £50

Charging order

To issue an application   £50

Warrant of possession or warrant of delivery

To issue an application   £80

Attachment of earnings

To issue an application order   £50

Oral examination

To issue an application   £40

Copies of documents

For first 5 photocopies   £1 per sheet

For subsequent copies   25p per sheet

Registration of county court judgments

To ask for a certificate of satisfaction or cancellation when a debt is paid   £10

Bankruptcy and company winding up

To issue a bankruptcy petition for your own
affairs (debtor's petition)   £120

To issue a bankruptcy petition against
someone who owes you money (creditor's
petition)   £150

To issue a petition to wind up a company that
owes you money   £150

To set aside a statutory demand   No Fee

Administration order

To issue a petition for an administration order   £100

The High Court

To issue a claim

To issue a claim where the claim is for
money only and the amount of the claim is
not more than:

    £50,000   £300

    Over £50,000   £400

If you are making a counterclaim, you must
pay a fee according to the above. For example,
if your counterclaim is for £20,000 you must
pay £300.

General fees

On the filing of an allocation questionnaire
by the claimant   £80

On the filing of a listing questionnaire or where
the court fixes the trial date or trial week
without the need for a listing questionnaire   £400

On filing notice of an appeal	£100
On an application by consent or without notice for a judgment or order where no other fee is specified	£25
On an application to vary a judgment or suspend enforcement	£25

Enforcing judgments

Writ of execution (High Court Sheriff)

To issue an application	£20

Writ of possession or writ of delivery

To issue an application	£20

Garnishee order

To issue an application	£50

Receiver

To issue an application	£50

Charging order

To issue an application	£50

Oral examination

To issue an application	£40

Bankruptcy and company winding up

To issue a bankruptcy petition for your own affairs (debtor's petition)	£120
To issue a bankruptcy petition against someone who owes you money (creditor's petition)	£150
To issue a petition to wind up a company that owes you money	£150
To set aside a statutory demand	No Fee

appendix D

Forms and letters used in this Desktop Guide

Forms and letters used in this Desktop Guide

This appendix will consist of a repeat of the following forms and letters used elsewhere:

- Example of a good application form for a credit account – (from Chapter 4).

- Example of a good request for a trade reference – (from Chapter 4).

- Example of a good first standard letter – (from Chapter 6).

- Example of a good second standard letter – (from Chapter 6).

- Example of a good final warning letter – (from Chapter 6).

- Front side of a completed claim form* – (from Chapter 17).

- Rear side of a completed claim form* – (from Chapter 17).

- Front side of notes for claimant on completing a claim form* – (from Chapter 17).

- Rear side of notes for claimant on completing a claim form* – (from Chapter 17).

- Example of a completed request for a warrant of execution* – (from Chapter 18).

- First page of a statutory demand form* – (from Chapter 19).

- Further page of a statutory demand form* – (from Chapter 19).

- Example of a good letter notifying a customer of a claim for bad debt relief – (from Chapter 20).

Crown copyright is reproduced with the permission of the Controller of Her Majesty's Stationery Office.

Example of a good application form for credit account

To: J Perkins Ltd
      14 King Street
      Hertford

Dear Sir

We request you to open a credit account in the name of:

_____

Address _____

_____

We accept that all invoices are payable within 30 days of date of issue. We have read your standard conditions of sale and agree that they will govern all trading between us. The maximum amount of credit required is expected to be £_____

Details of two trade referees are given below and we authorise you to make the normal enquiries of them.

Signature _____

Name _____

Position _____

Referee 1

Name _____

Address_____

_____

_____

Referee 2

Name _____

Address_____

_____

_____

Example of a good request for a trade reference

PRIVATE AND CONFIDENTIAL

Dear Sir

J R Smith Ltd of 2, Chiltern Street, Luton

The above has given your name as a trade reference. We would be grateful if you would answer the questions at the foot of this letter and return it in the enclosed prepaid envelope.

Your reply will be treated in strict confidence and at any time we will be pleased to respond to a similar request from yourselves.

Yours faithfully

W Brown
Credit Controller

How long has the above named traded with you?_____

What is the highest credit allowed? £ _____

What are your payment terms?_____

Is payment normally Prompt/Slow/Very Slow

Do you recommend them for total credit of £ _____ Yes/No

Any other information that you think might be helpful.

_____

_____

_____

Example of a good first standard letter

J Jones Esq
Chief Accountant
Burns and Fish Ltd
38 Broad Street
Northampton

1 October 1998

Dear Mr Jones

We notice that a balance of £269.24 is overdue for payment. We are not aware of any reason why payment should not be made but please do let me have details if this is the case.

If your payment is on the way to us please accept our thanks. Otherwise could we please have your remittance by return.

Yours sincerely,

K Green
Credit Controller

Example of a good second standard letter

J Jones Esq
Chief Accountant
Burns and Fish Ltd
38 Broad Street
Northampton

10 October 1998

Dear Mr Jones

We cannot trace a reply to our letter of 1 October requesting payment of the overdue balance of £269.24.

If there is any reason why payment should not be made would you let us know by return. Otherwise as the account is now very overdue we must ask for immediate settlement.

Yours sincerely,

K Green
Credit Controller

Example of a good final warning letter

The Company Secretary
Burns and Fish Ltd
38 Broad Street
Northampton

20 October 1998

Dear Sir

Overdue Balance of £269.24

We notice with regret the above balance is still outstanding. Although we wrote on 1 October and 10 October we have received neither payment nor a reason why payment should not be made.

We must now tell you that we expect payment to be made by 27 October. If payment has not been received by that date we will pass the matter to our solicitors with instructions to commence legal proceedings. This will be done without further warning to you.

Yours faithfully

K Green
Credit Controller

cc Mr J Jones

Claim Form

In the	
AYLESBURY	
Claim No.	

Claimant

JONES AND BROWN (A FIRM)
47 HILL STREET
AYLESBURY
BUCKS
HP22 4LK

SEAL

Defendant(s)

W. FLOWERS LTD
22 BROAD STREET
LUTON
BEDFORDSHIRE
LU7 2AT
(COMPANY NUMBER 1314222)

Brief details of claim

THE CLAIM IS FOR THE PRICE OF GOODS
SOLD AND DELIVERED.
THE REMEDY SOUGHT IS PAYMENT IN FULL

Value

SPECIMEN

Defendant's name and address

W. FLOWERS LTD
22 BROAD STREET
LUTON
BEDFORDSHIRE
LU7 2AT
(COMPANY NUMBER 1314222)

	£
Amount claimed	10,200.00
Court fee	200.00
Solicitor's costs	/
Total amount	10,400.00
Issue date	1ST JUNE 1999

The court office at

is open between 10 am and 4 pm Monday to Friday. When corresponding with the court, please address forms or letters to the Court Manager and quote the claim number.

N1 Claim form (CPR Part 7) (4.99)

	Claim No.	

Particulars of Claim (attached)(to follow)

THE CLAIM IS FOR £10,000 BEING THE PRICE OF AN ORIGINAL WATERCOLOUR PAINTING BY JOHN WEST ENTITLED 'RED APPLES' SOLD AND DELIVERED BY THE CLAIMANT TO THE DEFENDANT ON 1ST MARCH 1999, AND FOR INTEREST ON THAT SUM UNDER S69 COUNTY COURTS ACT 1984. THE CLAIMANT CLAIMS:

1 -   £10,000.00

2. INTEREST UNDER S69 COUNTY COURTS ACT 1984 AT THE RATE OF 8% PER YEAR AMOUNTING TO £200.00 FROM 1ST MARCH 1999. THE TOTAL NOW DUE IS £10,200.00 (IE £10,000 PLUS £200.00 INTEREST)

3. INTEREST AS ABOVE FROM 1ST JUNE 1999 AT THE RATE OF £2.19 DAILY UNTIL JUDGMENT OR EARLIER PAYMENT.

SPECIMEN

Statement of Truth
*(I believe)(The Claimant believes) that the facts stated in these particulars of claim are true.
* I am duly authorised by the claimant to sign this statement

Full name ___KEITH JOHN BROWN___

Name of claimant's solicitor's firm _____

signed___K. J. Brown___ position or office held _PARTNER_

*(Claimant)(Litigation friend)(Claimant's solicitor) (if signing on behalf of firm or company)
*delete as appropriate

Claimant's or claimant's solicitor's address to which documents or payments should be sent if different from overleaf including (if appropriate) details of DX, fax or e-mail.

Notes for claimant on completing a claim form

Further information may be obtained from the court in a series of free leaflets.

- Please read all of these guidance notes before you begin completing the claim form. The notes follow the order in which information is required on the form.
- Court staff can help you fill in the claim form and give information about procedure once it has been issued. But they cannot give legal advice. If you need legal advice, for example, about the likely success of your claim or the evidence you need to prove it, you should contact a solicitor or a Citizens Advice Bureau.
- If you are filling in the claim form by hand, please use black ink and write in block capitals.
- Copy the completed claim form and the defendant's notes for guidance so that you have one copy for yourself, one copy for the court and one copy for each defendant. Send or take the forms to the court office with the appropriate fee. The court will tell you how much this is.

Notes on completing the claim form

Heading

You must fill in the heading of the form to indicate whether you want the claim to be issued in a county court or in the High Court (The High Court means either a District Registry (attached to a county court) or the Royal Courts of Justice in London). There are restrictions on claims which may be issued in the High Court (see 'Value' overleaf).

Use whichever of the following is appropriate:

'In the ....County Court'
(inserting the name of the court)

or

'In the High Court of Justice.........................Division'
(inserting eg. 'Queen's Bench' or 'Chancery' as appropriate)
'.............................District Registry'
(inserting the name of the District Registry)

or

'In the High Court of Justice.........................Division,
(inserting eg. 'Queen's Bench' or 'Chancery' as appropriate)
Royal Courts of Justice'

Claimant and defendant details

As the person issuing the claim, you are called the 'claimant'; the person you are suing is called the 'defendant'. Claimants who are under 18 years old (unless otherwise permitted by the court) and patients within the meaning of the Mental Health Act 1983, must have a litigation friend to issue and conduct court proceedings on their behalf. Court staff will tell you more about what you need to do if this applies to you.

You must provide the following information about yourself **and** the defendant according to the capacity in which you are suing and in which the defendant is being sued. When suing or being sued as:-

an individual:

All known forenames and surname, whether Mr, Mrs, Miss, Ms or Other (e.g. Dr) and residential address (**including** postcode and telephone number) in England and Wales. Where the defendant is a proprietor of a business, a partner in a firm or an individual sued in the name of a club or other unincorporated association, the address for service should be the usual or last known place of residence **or** principal place of business of the company, firm or club or other unincorporated association.

Where the individual is:

under 18 write '(a child by Mr Joe Bloggs his litigation friend)' after the name. If the child is conducting proceedings on their own behalf write '(a child)' after the child's name.

a patient within the meaning of the Mental Health Act 1983 write '(by Mr Joe Bloggs his litigation friend)' after the patient's name.

trading under another name

you must add the words 'trading as' and the trading name e.g. 'Mr John Smith trading as Smith's Groceries'.

suing or being sued in a representative capacity

you must say what that capacity is e.g. 'Mr Joe Bloggs as the representative of Mrs Sharon Bloggs (deceased)'.

suing or being sued in the name of a club or other unincorporated association

add the words 'suing/sued on behalf of' followed by the name of the club or other unincorporated association.

a firm

enter the name of the firm followed by the words 'a firm' e.g. 'Bandbox - a firm' and an address for service which is either a partner's residential address or the principal or last known place of business.

a corporation (other than a company)

enter the full name of the corporation and the address which is either its principal office **or** any other place where the corporation carries on activities and which has a real connection with the claim.

a company registered in England and Wales

enter the name of the company and an address which is either the company's registered office **or** any place of business that has a real, or the most, connection with the claim e.g. the shop where the goods were bought.

an overseas company (defined by s744 of the Companies Act 1985)

enter the name of the company and either the address registered under s691 of the Act **or** the address of the place of business having a real, or the most, connection with the claim.

N1A Notes for claimant (4.99)

Brief details of claim

Note: The facts and full details about your claim and whether or not you are claiming interest, should be set out in the 'particulars of claim' *(see note under 'Particulars of Claim').*

You must set out under **this** heading:

- a concise statement of the nature of your claim
- the remedy you are seeking e.g. payment of money; an order for return of goods or their value; an order to prevent a person doing an act; damages for personal injuries.

Value

If you are claiming a **fixed amount of money** (a 'specified amount') write the amount in the box at the bottom right-hand corner of the claim form against 'amount claimed'.

If you are <u>not</u> claiming a fixed amount of money (an 'unspecified amount') under 'Value' write "I expect to recover" followed by whichever of the following applies to your claim:

- "not more than £5,000" **or**
- "more than £5,000 but not more than £15,000" **or**
- "more than £15,000"

If you are **not able** to put a value on your claim, write "I cannot say how much I expect to recover".

Personal injuries

If your claim is for 'not more than £5,000' and includes a claim for personal injuries, you must also write "My claim includes a claim for personal injuries and the amount I expect to recover as damages for pain, suffering and loss of amenity is" followed by either:

- "not more than £1,000" **or**
- "more than £1,000"

Housing disrepair

If your claim is for 'not more than £5,000' and includes a claim for housing disrepair relating to residential premises, you must also write "My claim includes a claim against my landlord for housing disrepair relating to residential premises. The cost of the repairs or other work is estimated to be" followed by either:

- "not more than £1,000" **or**
- "more than £1,000"

If within this claim, you are making a claim for other damages, you must also write:

"I expect to recover as damages" followed by either:

- "not more than £1,000" **or**
- "more than £1,000"

Issuing in the High Court

You may only issue in the High Court if one of the following statements applies to your claim:-

"By law, my claim must be issued in the High Court. The Act which provides this is ....(specify Act)"

or

"I expect to recover more than £15,000"

or

"My claim includes a claim for personal injuries and the value of the claim is £50,000 or more"

or

"My claim needs to be in a specialist High Court list, namely..................................(state which list)".

If one of the statements does apply and you wish to, or must by law, issue your claim in the High Court, write the words "I wish my claim to issue in the High Court because" followed by the relevant statement e.g. "I wish my claim to issue in the High Court because my claim includes a claim for personal injuries and the value of my claim is £50,000 or more."

Defendant's name and address

Enter in this box the full names and address of the defendant receiving the claim form (ie. one claim form for each defendant). If the defendant is to be served outside England and Wales, you may need to obtain the court's permission.

Particulars of claim

You may include your particulars of claim on the claim form in the space provided or in a separate document which you should head 'Particulars of Claim'. It should include the names of the parties, the court, the claim number and your address for service and also contain a statement of truth. You should keep a copy for yourself, provide one for the court and one for each defendant. Separate particulars of claim can either be served

- with the claim form **or**
- within 14 days after the date on which the claim form was served.

If your particulars of claim are served separately from the claim form, they must be served with the forms on which the defendant may reply to your claim.

Your particulars of claim must include

- a concise statement of the facts on which you rely
- a statement (if applicable) to the effect that you are seeking aggravated damages or exemplary damages
- details of any interest which you are claiming
- any other matters required for your type of claim as set out in the relevant practice direction

Address for documents

Insert in this box the address at which you wish to receive documents and/or payments, if different from the address you have already given under the heading 'Claimant'. The address must be in England or Wales. If you are willing to accept service by DX, fax or e-mail, add details.

Statement of truth

This must be signed by you, by your solicitor or your litigation friend, as appropriate.

Where the claimant is a registered company or a corporation the claim must be signed by either the director, treasurer, secretary, chief executive, manager or other officer of the company or (in the case of a corporation) the mayor, chairman, president or town clerk.

Request for Warrant of Execution

to be completed and signed by the plaintiff or his solicitor and sent to the court with the appropriate fee

1 Plaintiff's name and address

JONES AND BROWN (A FIRM)
47 HILL STREET
AYLESBURY
BUCKS
HP22 4LK

In the

AYLESBURY **County Court**

Case Number 45 31313

2 Name and address for service and payment (if different from above)
Ref/Tel No.

0129-611 111

3 Defendant's name and address

MRS MAVIS SMITH
18 JUNIPER ROAD
AYLESBURY
BUCKS
HP22 7...

SPECIMEN

4 Warrant details

(A) Balance due at date of this request	600	00
(B) Amount for which warrant to issue	600	00
Issue fee	40	00
Solicitor's costs		
Land Registry fee		
TOTAL	640	00

If the amount of the warrant at (B) is less than the balance at (A), the sum due after the warrant is paid will be

I certify that the whole or part of any instalments due under the judgment or order have not been paid and the balance now due is as shown

Signed L. Brown (PARTNER)

Plaintiff (Plaintiff's solicitor)

Dated AUGUST 18ᵗʰ 1988

IMPORTANT
You must inform the court immediately of any payments you receive after you have sent this request to the court

---

Other information that might assist the bailiff including the name(s) and address(es) of any 2nd/3rd defendant and other address(es) at which the defendant might have goods. You should also tell the court if you have reason to believe that the bailiff might encounter serious difficulties in attempting to execute the warrant.

MRS SMITH OWNS A BLUE BMW 525 CAR REGISTRATION NUMBER H136 SRO. IT IS KEPT IN THE GARAGE AT THE REAR OF HER HOUSE.

Warrant No.

N323 *Request for warrant of execution (Order 26, rule 1(1)) (5.95)*   Reproduced by Law Pack Publishing with the permission of the Controller of HMSO

Form 6.2

Statutory Demand
under section 268(1)(a)
of the Insolvency
Act 1986.
Debt for Liquidated
Sum Payable
Immediately
Following a Judgment
or Order of the Court
(Rule 6.7)

NOTES FOR CREDITOR
- If the Creditor is entitled to the debt by way of assignment, details of the original Creditor and any intermediary assignees should be given in part C on page 3.
- If the amount of debt includes interest not previously notified to the Debtor as included in the Debtor's liability, details should be given, including the grounds upon which interest is charged. The amount of interest must be shown separately.
- Any other charge accruing due from time to time may be claimed. The amount or rate of the charge must be identified and the grounds on which it is claimed must be stated.
- In either case the amount claimed must be limited to that which has accrued due at the date of the Demand.
- If the Creditor holds any security the amount of debt should be the sum the Creditor is prepared to regard as unsecured for the purposes of this Demand. Brief details of the total debt should be included and the nature of the security and the value put upon it by the Creditor, as at the date of the Demand, must be specified.
- Details of the judgment or order should be inserted, including details of the Division of the Court or District Registry and Court reference, where judgment is obtained in the High Court.
- If signatory of the Demand is a solicitor or other agent of the Creditor, the name of his/her firm should be given.

* Delete if signed by the Creditor himself.

WARNING

- This is an **important** document. You should refer to the notes entitled "How to comply with a Statutory Demand or have it set aside".
- If you wish to have this Demand set aside you must make application to do so **within 18 days** from its service on you.
- If you do not apply to set aside **within 18 days** or otherwise deal with this Demand as set out in the notes **within 21 days** after its service on you, you could be made bankrupt and your property and goods taken away from you.
- Please read the Demand and notes carefully. If you are in any doubt about your position you should seek advice **immediately** from a solicitor or your nearest Citizens Advice Bureau.

DEMAND

To

Address

SPECIMEN

This Demand is served on you by the Creditor:

Name

Address

The Creditor claims that you owe the sum of £   ,
full particulars of which are set out on page 2, and that it is payable immediately and, to the extent of the sum demanded, is unsecured.

By a Judgment /Order of the High Court   /
                                                County Court in proceedings entitled

(Case) Number   between

                                                                        Plaintiff

and   Defendant

it was adjudged/ordered that you pay to the Creditor the sum of £
and £   for costs.

The Creditor demands that you pay the above debt or secure or compound for it to the Creditor's satisfaction.

[The Creditor making this Demand is a Minister of the Crown or a Government Department, and it is intended to present a Bankruptcy Petition in the High Court in London.] [Delete if inappropriate].

Signature of individual

Name
(BLOCK LETTERS)

Date   day of   19

*Position with or relationship to Creditor:
*I am authorised to make this Demand on the Creditor's behalf.

Address

Tel. No.   Ref. No.

N.B. The person making this Demand must complete the whole of pages 1, 2 and parts A, B and C (as applicable) on page 3.

[P.T.O.

Part A

Appropriate Court for Setting Aside Demand

Rule 6.4(2) of the Insolvency Rules 1986 states that the appropriate Court is the Court to which you would have to present your own Bankruptcy Petition in accordance with Rule 6.40(1) and 6.40(2).

Any application by you to set aside this Demand should be made to that Court, or, if this Demand is issued by a Minister of the Crown or a Government Department, you must apply to the High Court to set aside if it is intended to present a Bankruptcy Petition against you in the High Court (see page 1).

In accordance with those rules on present information the appropriate Court is [the High Court of Justice] [County Court]
(address)

Part B

The individual or individuals to whom any communication regarding this Demand may be addressed is/are:
Name...
(BLOCK LETTERS)

Address...

....

Telephone Number...

Reference...

Part C

For completion if the Creditor is entitled to the debt by way of assignment.

	Name	Date(s) of Assignment
Original Creditor		
Assignees		

How to comply with a Statutory Demand or have it set aside (ACT WITHIN 18 DAYS)

If you wish to avoid a Bankruptcy Petition being presented against you, you must pay the debt shown on page 1, particulars of which are set out on page 2 of this notice, within the period of **21 days** after its service upon you. However, if the Demand follows (includes) a Judgment or Order of a County Court, any payment must be made to that County Court (quoting the Case No.). Alternatively, you can attempt to come to a settlement with the Creditor. To do this you should:

• inform the individual (or one of the individuals) named in Part B above immediately that you are willing and able to offer security for the debt to the Creditor's satisfaction; or
• inform the individual (or one of the individuals) named in Part B above immediately that you are willing and able to compound for the debt to the Creditor's satisfaction.

If you dispute the Demand in whole or in part you should:
• contact the individual (or one of the individuals) named in Part B immediately.

If you consider that you have grounds to have this Demand set aside or if you do not quickly receive a satisfactory written reply from the individual named in Part B whom you have contacted you should **apply within 18 days** from the date of service of this Demand on you to the appropriate Court shown in Part A above to have the Demand set aside.

Any application to set aside the Demand (Form 6.4 in Schedule 4 of the Insolvency Rules 1986) should be made within 18 days from the date of service upon you and be supported by an Affidavit (Form 6.5 in Schedule 4 to those Rules) stating the grounds on which the Demand should be set aside. The forms may be obtained from the appropriate Court when you attend to make the application.

> **Remember:** From the date of service on you of this document:
> (a) you have only **18 days** to apply to the Court to have the Demand set aside, and
> (b) you have only **21 days** before the Creditor may present a Bankruptcy Petition.

3

Example of a good letter notifying a customer of a claim for VAT bad debt relief

The Company Secretary
Bladon Software Ltd
18 Croft Street
Witney
Oxfordshire

December 19 1998

Dear Sir

Notification of Report to Customs and Excise

As required by law, I am writing to notify you that you have been reported to Customs and Excise. This company has claimed VAT bad debt relief of £1,750.00 in respect of our valid invoice number 12354 to you for £11,750.00 dated December 22 1997.

If you have claimed a deduction of £1,750.00 on this invoice, you may be required by law to repay it. Customs and Excise may require to inspect all records relating to this transaction, may check to see that repayment of the VAT has been made, and may conduct a general inspection of your VAT records.

This company has not abandoned its claim to payment of £11,750.00. It is our intention to vigorously pursue payment and instigate legal proceedings.

Yours faithfully

P Patel
Credit Controller

Thorogood publishing

Thorogood publishes a wide range of books, reports, special briefings, psychometric tests and videos. Listed below is a selection of key titles.

Desktop Guides

The marketing strategy desktop guide
Norton Paley • £16.99

The sales manager's desktop guide
Mike Gale and Julian Clay • £16.99

The company director's desktop guide
David Martin • £16.99

The credit controller's desktop guide
Roger Mason • £16.99

The company secretary's desktop guide
Roger Mason • £16.99

The finance and accountancy desktop guide
Ralph Tiffin • £16.99

The commercial engineer's desktop guide
Tim Boyce • £16.99

The training manager's desktop guide
Eddie Davies • £16.99

The PR practitioner's desktop guide
Caroline Black • £16.99

Win new business - the desktop guide
Susan Croft • £16.99

Masters in Management

Mastering business planning and strategy
Paul Elkin • £14.99

Mastering financial management
Stephen Brookson • £14.99

Mastering leadership   *Michael Williams* • £14.99

Mastering marketing   *Ian Ruskin-Brown* • £16.99

Mastering negotiations   *Eric Evans* • £14.99

Mastering people management
Mark Thomas • £14.99

Mastering personal and interpersonal skills
Peter Haddon • £14.99

Mastering project management
Cathy Lake • £14.99

Business Action Pocketbooks

Edited by David Irwin

Building your business pocketbook	£6.99
Developing yourself and your staff pocketbook	£6.99
Finance and profitability pocketbook	£6.99
Managing and employing people pocketbook	£6.99
Sales and marketing pocketbook	£6.99
Managing projects and operations pocketbook	£6.99
Effective business communications pocketbook	£6.99

PR techniques that work
Edited by Jim Dunn • £6.99

Adair on leadership
Edited by Neil Thomas • £6.99m

Other titles

The complete guide to debt recovery
Roger Mason • £12.99

The John Adair handbook of management and leadership
Edited by Neil Thomas • £12.99

The inside track to successful management
Dr Gerald Kushel • £12.99

The pension trustee's handbook
(3rd edition)   *Robin Ellison* • £25

Boost your company's profits
Barrie Pearson • £12.99

Negotiate to succeed   *Julie Lewthwaite* • £12.99

The management tool kit   *Sultan Kermally* • £10.99

Working smarter   *Graham Roberts-Phelps* • £14.99

Test your management skills
Michael Williams • £15.99

The art of headless chicken management
Elly Brewer and Mark Edwards • £6.99

Everything you need for an NVQ in management
Julie Lewthwaite • £22.99

Customer relationship management
Graham Roberts-Phelps • £14.99

Sales management and organisation
Peter Green • £10.99

Telephone tactics   *Graham Roberts-Phelps* • £10.99

Companies don't succeed people do!
Graham Roberts-Phelps • £12.99

Inspiring leadership   *John Adair* • £15.99

The book of Me
Barrie Pearson and Neil Thomas • £14.99

The complete guide to debt recovery
Roger Mason • £12.99

Dynamic practice development
Kim Tasso • £19.99

Gurus on business strategy   *Tony Grundy* • £14.99

The concise Adair on leadership
Edited by Neil Thomas • £9.99

The concise time management and personal
development   *Adair and Melanie Allen* • £9.99

Successful selling solutions   *Julian Clay* • £12.99

Gurus on marketing   *Sultan Kermally* • £14.99

The concise Adair on communication and
presentation skills   *Edited by Neil Thomas* • £9.99

High performance consulting skills
Mark Thomas • £15.99

Developing and managing talent
Sultan Kermally • £14.99

Thorogood also has an extensive range of reports and special briefings which are written specifically for professionals wanting expert information.

For a full listing of all Thorogood publications, or to order any title, please call Thorogood Customer Services on 020 7749 4748 or fax on 020 7729 6110. Alternatively view our website at **www.thorogood.ws**.

Focused on developing your potential

Falconbury, the sister company to Thorogood publishing, brings together the leading experts from all areas of management and strategic development to provide you with a comprehensive portfolio of action-centred training and learning.

We understand everything managers and leaders need to be, know and do to succeed in today's commercial environment. Each product addresses a different technical or personal development need that will encourage growth and increase your potential for success.

- Practical public training programmes
- Tailored in-company training
- Coaching
- Mentoring
- Topical business seminars
- Trainer bureau/bank
- Adair Leadership Foundation

The most valuable resource in any organisation is its people; it is essential that you invest in the development

of your management and leadership skills to ensure your team fulfil their potential. Investment into both personal and professional development has been proven to provide an outstanding ROI through increased productivity in both you and your team. Ultimately leading to a dramatic impact on the bottom line.

With this in mind Falconbury have developed a comprehensive portfolio of training programmes to enable managers of all levels to develop their skills in leadership, communications, finance, people management, change management and all areas vital to achieving success in today's commercial environment.

What Falconbury can offer you?

- Practical applied methodology with a proven results
- Extensive bank of experienced trainers
- Limited attendees to ensure one-to-one guidance

- Up to the minute thinking on management and leadership techniques
- Interactive training
- Balanced mix of theoretical and practical learning
- Learner-centred training
- Excellent cost/quality ratio

Falconbury In-Company Training

Falconbury are aware that a public programme may not be the solution to leadership and management issues arising in your firm. Involving only attendees from your organisation and tailoring the programme to focus on the current challenges you face individually and as a business may be more appropriate. With this in mind we have brought together our most motivated and forward thinking trainers to deliver tailored in-company programmes developed specifically around the needs within your organisation.

All our trainers have a practical commercial background and highly refined people skills. During the course of the programme they act as facilitator, trainer and mentor, adapting their style to ensure that each individual benefits equally from their knowledge to develop new skills.

Falconbury works with each organisation to develop a programme of training that fits your needs.

Mentoring and coaching

Developing and achieving your personal objectives in the workplace is becoming increasingly difficult in today's constantly changing environment. Additionally, as a manager or leader, you are responsible for guiding colleagues towards the realisation of their goals. Sometimes it is easy to lose focus on your short and long-term aims.

Falconbury's one-to-one coaching draws out individual potential by raising self-awareness and understanding, facilitating the learning and performance development that creates excellent managers and leaders. It builds renewed self-confidence and a strong sense of 'can-do' competence, contributing significant benefit to the organisation. Enabling you to focus your energy on developing your potential and that of your colleagues.

Mentoring involves formulating winning strategies, setting goals, monitoring achievements and motivating the whole team whilst achieving a much improved work life balance.

Falconbury – Business Legal Seminars

Falconbury Business Legal Seminars specialises in the provision of high quality training for legal professionals from both in-house and private practice internationally.

The focus of these events is to provide comprehensive and practical training on current international legal thinking and practice in a clear and informative format.

Event subjects include, drafting commercial agreements, employment law, competition law, intellectual property, managing an in-house legal department and international acquisitions.

For more information on all our services please contact Falconbury on +44 (0) 20 7729 6677 or visit the website at: www.falconbury.co.uk.